MONEY MASTERY

IN JUST MINUTES A DAY

Fred E. Waddell

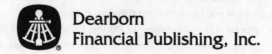

Dearborn
Financial Publishing, Inc.

This publication is designed to provide accurate and authoritative information in regard to the subject matter covered. It is sold with the understanding that the publisher is not engaged in rendering legal, accounting or other professional service. If legal advice or other expert assistance is required, the services of a competent professional person should be sought.

Acquisitions Editor: Christine E. Litavsky
Managing Editor: Jack Kiburz
Interior Design: Elizandro Carrington
Cover Design: DePinto Studios

Published by Dearborn Financial Publishing, Inc.®

Printed in the United States of America

96 97 98 10 9 8 7 6 5 4 3 2 1

Library of Congress Cataloging-in-Publication Data

Waddell, Fred E.
    Money mastery in just minutes a day / Fred E. Waddell.
      p. cm.
    Includes bibliographical references and index.
    ISBN 0-7931-2299-6 (pbk.)
    1. Finance, Personal—Planning. 2. Finance, Personal—
Psychological aspects. 3. Money—Psychological aspects.
I. Title.
HG179.W23 1996
332.024—dc20   96-13860
                                    CIP

Dearborn books are available at special quantity discounts to use as premiums and sales promotions, or for use in corporate training programs. For more information, please call the Special Sales Manager at 800-621-9621, ext. 4384, or write to Dearborn Financial Publishing, Inc., 155 N. Wacker Dr., Chicago, IL 60606-1719.

DEDICATION

This book is dedicated with love to my daughter, Kristin Anne Kapfer, and to my son, Todd Spaulding Waddell.

CONTENTS

PREFACE

Congratulations! Purchasing this book reveals your personal commitment to mastering your finances. Doing so has never been this simple. Not only does this book show you what to do, but also how to do it. It describes a simple yet effective program—requiring just minutes a day—that will empower you to master your money for life. It pulls together the essentials to get you on track and headed in the right direction and provides a gentle push to get you started.

This handy guide was written with procrastinators in mind. It not only shows you what to do, it also focuses on helping you do what you already know. You will discover that you have more money smarts and more resources—both financial and personal—than you realize. You simply need to become more aware of your resources and learn how to organize them in more productive and useful ways. The book will help you overcome any fears, worries, doubts, personal conflicts and ambivalence that may have caused you to procrastinate. You'll find that your confidence will improve along with your competence.

This book is much different from other books you might have read on managing your money. The first part of the book focuses your attention on helping you reexamine your financial life and empowering you to overcome any beliefs or habits that may have prevented you from improving it. The second part of the book guides you through a process of self-assessment and then helps you develop a simple but effective plan of action.

One of the many unique features of this book is the action plan, which combines dynamic money management principles with significant breakthroughs in human behavior research, Solution Focused Brief Therapy and Neuro-Linguistic Programming™ (NLP). I describe small key steps, which can be done in just minutes a day and can result in fundamental lifelong improvements.

The techniques described in this book are the same ones that I have used successfully with clients, which enabled them to turn their financial lives around in just one or two counseling sessions. I have taught these skills to over 4,000 financial counselors and therapists in the United States and Canada, who also report that they are very effective! They will work for you too as you apply them to your own life. So, as you read this book and apply the simple concepts, remember to enjoy yourself and to acknowledge your growing confidence, competence, self-esteem and peace of mind!

Acknowledgments

A book manuscript on an important issue like this is not written; it evolves, often over many years. It's much like giving birth with frequent labor pains, not just those of the writer, but of many people who contribute in many ways. This book would not have been possible without the extensive input and labor of my wife, Beverly Barrett. Her continual suggestions, excellent computer skills and constant encouragement were as much a part of the evolution of this book as my writing it. A special note of thanks is also due to Caroline Carney, former editor-in-chief; Christine Litavsky, my current editor at Dearborn, whose enthusiasm for this book and its positive potential for readers were an added incentive; and to Sue Telingator, whose superb editing of this manuscript made it more readable. To the many clients and participants in my Solution Focused Financial Counseling seminars, I owe my deepest gratitude for what *they have taught me! I pray that I have been able to teach them something as well!* Appreciation is also extended to Elizabeth A. Edwards for allowing us to use her compulsive consumer buying behavior measurement; to my mother, whose unshakable faith in me throughout my life let me know that I can accomplish anything when I make up my mind to do so!; and to my friends, Bernie Cleveland, Scott Simpson and Bill Way, whose relentlessly positive attitudes and encouragement have been an inspiration for me and for others in the fields of education and financial counseling. Last, but not least, a special acknowledgment goes to my two dogs, Scruffy and Ragmuffin, simply two "Harriett-bred" mixed-breed mutts, who at the end of each day remind me with wagging tails and face licks that no matter what happens, it's going to be okay!

PART ONE

UNDERSTANDING AND CONQUERING YOUR FINANCIAL ATTITUDES

1.

YOUR FINANCIAL ATTITUDES AND HABITS

I have three treasures:
Love, frugality and humility.
Having love, I can be courageous.
Being frugal, I can afford to be generous.
Being humble, I can learn the wisdom of the world.

—Tao Te Ching

Most books on personal money management provide financial information and advice on how to handle your money. I've spent the past 30 years as a financial counselor, a trainer of financial counselors and a university professor of family money management. My experience has shown me that many people aren't in control of their money and don't feel financially secure. This is because they not only don't know what to do, but also because they don't *do* what they know.

Excuses abound! How often do you hear people speak about their financial lives with these clichés?

- "I'm too busy."

- "I'll get around to it later."

- "Money matters are just not my thing; I'll leave them to the experts."

- "We're free spirits; we spend spontaneously when we have it and don't spend when we don't have it. It's as simple as that."

- "It's impossible to plan during these unstable, unpredictable times."

- "Things will just happen as they were meant to; there's no point in worrying about them."
- "It's all in the hands of God anyway, so why be concerned about it?"

The problem is that these kinds of clichés don't help. They don't prevent financial problems from happening, nor do they prevent the inevitable worry that accompanies such problems. They don't produce financial security; they don't enable people to handle the inevitable financial emergencies that are a normal part of life; they don't enable people to do what they really want to do and be what they really want to be; and they certainly—most importantly—don't produce peace of mind! "Money matters are just not my thing?"—that's like saying, personal hygiene is just not my thing. No one has to become an expert, but all of us have to know enough to care for ourselves and our loved ones and to enjoy a modest amount of prosperity and peace of mind. Here is the point of this book: Financial well-being really is much simpler and takes much less time than so-called financial experts will tell you! You don't need an expert or a financial counselor. You can become your own financial counselor!

The three principles of financial prosperity are really quite simple:

1. Plan your financial journey through life just as you would plan any other trip.
2. Use the KISS formula: "Keep it short and simple!"
3. Pay attention to what's happening in your life.

If your life consists of dealing with one financial crisis after another, then you are creating or at least contributing to your own crises. This may sound harsh, but you are creating these crises by not financially preparing yourself in advance for their inevitability and by ignoring some very simple steps. This book will show you what you need to do and how you can do it in just minutes a day. Remember, it's not only what you know, but also what you do consistently—even if only for a few minutes a day—that's important. You brush your teeth every day for just a few minutes to prevent tooth problems. You don't say, "I'll just brush my teeth once a month, but for a much longer period of time." The program described in this book is just as simple and takes about as much time as brushing your teeth, and it's just as important that it be done with the same consistency.

YOUR CHILDHOOD PROGRAMMING

Mary Sloan and her husband Ted were referred to me by a local psychotherapist. Money issues were a recurring problem in their relationship. Like so many women today, Mary had grown up in a family where money issues were considered inappropriate topics for children or for family discussions. Whenever there was a question about insurance, mortgages, savings, budgeting or investing, her mother responded with, "I don't know about that; your father takes care of those matters. Come on, I'm feeling blue and bored today; let's go shopping." When Mary approached her father, who spent money freely and was just as free in giving her money when she asked for it, he responded in a scolding tone with, "Why are you asking me about this? Let me take care of the money issues in this house, and you take care of your schoolwork."

Sometimes late at night, Mary would hear her mother and father arguing over some money matter. Once she even told her mother how inadequate she felt about such things and how she wished she knew more. Her mother responded with, "There's plenty of time for that later; you'll pick that up as you go through life. Besides, with a little luck, you'll find someone like your father who will be responsible for those things, and you won't have to worry about them."

Mary went on to college, met Ted and married right after graduating. As they began to plan their life together, money matters naturally arose. She found that Ted had values that were much different from her own. Ted grew up in a family where his father had used money to reward and to punish. His father was tight-fisted and used money to get his way, withholding it when he was displeased with anyone in the house and loosening the purse strings a little if everything went his way. When Ted brought up the subject of money, his father would admonish him by saying, "Well, money doesn't grow on trees." This was the extent of Ted's money-management training by his family. His father refused to discuss the subject, saying it was his job as the man of the house to deal with money matters and none of anyone else's business. He was also concerned that his kids not tell others about their family business.

Whenever the subject of money came up in their marriage, Mary and Ted were clearly uncomfortable, associating any discussions with starting an argument. They approached money from a fight-or-flight stance, usually preferring to avoid the subject altogether. There was an uneasy calm in their relationship that came from trying to avoid discussing money, but they also both realized that money matters could not be avoided. They had no savings since they had no financial goals. They simply spent everything they made as they made it. When unexpected financial emergencies arose, such as a needed repair or replacement, they blamed each other for the emergency.

Mary and Ted were always "maxed out" on their credit cards and simply applied for new ones or for consolidation loans to pay for their ever-mounting bills. Then Mary got pregnant and had to stop working for a while. Financial emergencies became crises, and occasional money squabbles became more frequent and more vicious as each accused the other of being irresponsible and uncommunicative.

When I saw them in my office, Mary stared out the window as Ted proudly boasted of his accomplishments at work and his recent raise. When I asked him what he planned to do with the additional money, he began listing all of the things that "we" planned to buy. Mary turned beet red, glared at him and then said to me, "He always does that. He's constantly looking for new things to buy without asking me first." Ted replied, "Why should I ask you? You admit to not knowing anything about money matters and have said that you don't want to know either."

It became clear to me where each of them had gotten their viewpoints and their approaches to money. Their attitudes and words were exactly what they had heard from their parents while growing up. Also, I could hear the fear behind the words, because their inability to communicate about money was spilling over into their ability to communicate about other important issues. Their marriage would be in jeopardy unless they came to grips with this and learned to effectively communicate about money. They needed to understand how their parents' messages and models influenced their beliefs and did not adequately prepare them for their adult money responsibilities. They needed to understand their own and each other's money attitudes, habits, idiosyncrasies and underlying fears. And lastly, they needed to begin educating themselves about these matters.

People who have financial problems and are uncomfortable whenever the subject of money arises, often have fears or other negative feelings about money. These fears can be traced to childhood, and they may find that their limited thinking comes from parental programming or beliefs. At a very early age, the words, beliefs and unspoken messages of their parents and others became fixed in their subconscious. Sometimes I ask my clients to take a moment to close their eyes and remember an event related to money. It will be the event about which they have the strongest feelings. In a matter of seconds, they remember an event from childhood. It may have lasted only a few minutes, but it has had an impact on their lives, as well as their beliefs and feelings about money since then, including their view of financial roles and responsibilities, how money *should* be used and its place in their lives. This significant event from their childhood not only affects how they communicate with their spouse about money, but also whether such communication takes place at all.

Recognize the beliefs about money that you got from your parents and consciously decide if you want to keep them. Forgive your parents for any beliefs they may have taught you that no longer are useful to you. Realize that they did the best they could at the time. The beliefs they taught you might have been appropriate for you when you were younger. These beliefs may not be appropriate now that you are an adult, living in a more complex world and facing different circumstances. You can make wise choices and decisions on your own.

IDENTIFYING YOUR MONEY BELIEFS AND BLINDSPOTS

It is an interesting fact that it's harder for people to talk about their attitudes and habits with money than about any other aspect of their lives, including sex. People link their identity or personal self-image to money and how they handle it. They may even feel embarrassed about their money management abilities, particularly if they are experiencing financial problems. They label mistakes as failures and then generalize these so-called failures as statements about themselves and about their total effectiveness as adults.

Some people consider themselves to be free spirits. They say that they do not want to think about money and prefer to live in the here and now. In reality, they are closet worriers. These "free spirits" are never able to get ahead. Their entire lives are spent in a hand-to-mouth lifestyle. Then they complain about too much month left at the end of their money, while avoiding any planning for their future. Without planning, they ironically give up their freedom. If you do not control your money, then your money will control you. It tells you where you can go, what you can do and even how you can spend your time.

There are people who because they either faced severe deprivation as children or had parents who were constantly worried about money reflect this insecurity now as adults. They are the hoarders, unable to enjoy their money. Not only are they afraid to spend beyond the bare necessities, they tend to save in the most conservative way possible. Their savings are kept in passbook savings or in savings bonds, and they cannot accept any kind of risk, no matter how slight. Their use of money reflects their overall outlook that life is mean, brutish and short. When they somehow manage to get a few extra dollars, they can immediately think of some current or impending necessity for the money. When they purchase something, they purchase the least expensive one that they can find, then wonder if there might be an even cheaper one somewhere. Even when they are having fun, they are constantly watching the clock, worried about the financial effect of this extravagance. When a hoarder marries a spender, marital discord is inevitable and divorce likely. The Depression not only had a profound effect on those who lived through it, but it also affected their children.

In addition, an estimated one out of every five people has some problems controlling his or her spending. For half of them, spending is their "drug" of choice and is their usual way of dealing with emotional upset. Compulsive spending can lead to severe debt and other financial problems. It can end in bankruptcy, and the problems often do not end there. Four out of five people who file for bankruptcy are back in trouble within just five years. Money was never intended to be used as an emotional narcotic. As you will discover later in this book, there are numerous more fulfilling and less destructive ways of dealing with emotional highs and lows than by spending money. One of my clients, Mrs. Doe, was a typical compulsive spender.

When Mrs. Doe entered my office, she said with tears in her eyes, "I think I've got a problem; I hope you can help me." In her 40s, Mrs. Doe had been divorced for a few years from a lawyer with six-figure earnings. She said, "I just can't stop spending money." When I asked her how she knew that she had a spending problem, she related the following story to me: One Saturday evening, she was in her car on her way to a party. She was wearing a brand-new blouse that she had never worn before. While driving to the party, she looked down at her blouse and said to herself, "I don't like this blouse." She then drove miles out of her way to find a store that was open. She went in and bought not just one, but three new blouses, confiding that she also almost bought a cashmere sweater, but put it back when she reached the checkout counter. She had two daughters in college who did not live at home. Every day when she got off work, she would ask one or both daughters to go shopping with her, promising to buy them something to get them to go with her. She said to me with tears in her eyes, "I don't like going home to an empty house." She belonged to one of the most expensive country clubs in town and ate all of her evening meals there. Even after she saw how much she was spending in country club dues and dinners, she wouldn't give up her membership because it was her best chance of meeting another man. She was used to men taking care of her. She was an only child and her father had indulged her. Then her husband took care of her. She thought her best chance to get herself out from under all her debt was to find another man. She then reflected a moment and said, "But on the other hand, what man would ever want a woman with the kinds of debts I have?" On weekends, she said that she slept to almost noon, a reliable indicator of how bleak her life was and of her paralysis in dealing with it.

Truly, Mrs. Doe was in every sense of the word a compulsive spender. Her out-of-control spending had resulted in a huge amount of debt. Spending was, indeed, her drug of choice. It was her way of dealing with her obvious loneliness. Solving her problem was simple. First, we had to find ways of quickly interrupting her pattern of spending every time she felt lonely or blue. Then we had to find ways to deal with her loneliness other than spending money. These more empowering ways would enhance her self-esteem while giving her new choices and new ways of expressing herself, of having fun, of gaining attention and of feeling powerful and in control. I told her that the best way of attracting another man was to feel good about herself!

THE DIFFERENCE BETWEEN BELIEFS AND VALUES

There are plenty of books today on what to do with your money. What is equally important when it comes to money matters is what to do with your mind. Your beliefs about money ultimately determine what will happen to you financially. Beliefs, including self-limiting ones, can be quite powerful. For example, studies have shown that a sugar pill placebo labeled "Heavy Duty Pain Killer" had a much greater effect in reducing patients' pain than a morphine tablet labeled "Mild Pain Killer," and that patients reported feeling better just by watching their doctor write out a prescription. Self-limiting beliefs begin with the words *I can't* or other expressions of one's inability to do something. People often confuse their values with their beliefs, but there are important differences between the two.

Values are often stated in just one or two words, such as *honesty, loyalty, commitment* and *love.* They usually don't motivate people to act. You will find value words included in sentences such as, His honesty is above reproach. You can identify and rank a list of your values ranging from most important to least important. Values give focus to your life and define what you pay attention to. The following are examples of values you might use to describe yourself:

- Faithful
- Loving
- Loyal
- Committed
- Honest
- Truthful
- Trustworthy
- Person of integrity
- Healthy

Beliefs, on the other hand, are powerful motivators. Unlike values, they are stated only as complete sentences. They decide how you respond to daily occurrences and circumstances. Beliefs are more flexible and change more easily and rapidly than values. They change frequently as we mature, have new experiences and gain new education and information. Many things that we believed even a few years ago, we no longer believe today. Inflexible beliefs are self-limiting, disabling, disempowering, keep people stuck in ineffective patterns of behavior and are not values. We can change beliefs if we choose, and often quite easily. Here are a few examples of beliefs you might hold:

- "Always tithe at least 10 percent of your income to your church."
- "You get what you pay for."
- "You can't cheat an honest man."
- "Price determines quality."
- "Always buy the most expensive item you can find to get top quality."
- "Credit increases the amount of money a person has to spend."

YOUR BELIEFS CREATE YOUR REALITY

Your beliefs about money determine your financial reality. Because you create in your mind what you believe, you will have many experiences that reinforce your beliefs and prove to you that reality operates in the way you think it does. For example, someone who believes that money comes only from working hard will receive money only from hard work. You can change what you experience simply by changing what you believe. You must change what you believe if you really want to change what you have been experiencing.

Nancy Smith was a 29-year-old executive working for a large national corporation when she came to see me seeking confirmation that what she was doing financially was right or correct. In other words, like so many people with low self-esteem, she needed to have her money management habits validated by someone else. She made several references to having peaked out professionally, lamenting the fact that because she was a female, she had hit the so-called glass ceiling in her employment. This seemed strange to me because I knew someone else at the same company who said they were having trouble finding women to promote into upper management positions. I had also recently read an article about the company that indicated the same problem.

As we explored this issue, it became clear that the glass ceiling she referred to resulted from her own self-limiting beliefs. Deep down inside, she really believed that she had progressed professionally about as far as she was meant to. She believed that since she had come so far and had been so successful, then failure must be right around the corner. She said, "Why push the envelope and risk losing it all?" When I asked her what she meant by losing it all, she replied, "My job and my friends." When I asked her what adjustments she had made at work to reflect this belief, she began describing several things she was doing at work to become less visible (meaning less vulnerable in her mind). She volunteered less for new projects, spoke up less often and in general played it safe. It was easy to see how her boss could have interpreted this differently, such as her being less enthusiastic, less of a team player, less involved, less committed, less dynamic and so on. She had indeed created her own glass ceiling because of low self-esteem, possibly resulting from messages received during childhood.

For example, a common belief is that you will not be thought as lovable by others if you have money. You will only be loved for your money and not for yourself. People also sometimes worry that having money will somehow separate them from their friends. They may worry that having a large sum of money will become a burdensome responsibility and tie them down. Being burdened by financial responsibility is not possible unless people believe they will be and subconsciously set themselves up so that their beliefs come true. What they believe is what they create in their life.

Some people have conflicting beliefs that prevent them from becoming financially secure. For example, they may hold conflicting beliefs about what it would mean to have extra money beyond what is needed for bare necessities. To be financially secure, they must first resolve such inner conflicts and be clear about what steps they need to take and what habits they need to avoid. If they have mixed beliefs about what they should do, then their results will be mixed, at best, or they will procrastinate from taking any action at all.

If you tell yourself that money will give you more freedom, peace of mind and a chance to do things for people you love, while you believe that if you have extra money it would mean that you are materialistic and not spiritual, that someone else will have less if you have more or that the government will take most of it in taxes, then such conflicting beliefs will practically ensure that you do not become financially successful. By not resolving your conflicts, you unconsciously condition yourself to avoid taking the steps needed to obtain financial security and peace of mind.

It is important to understand that it matters little if your beliefs, habits or choices about money are right or wrong. What is important is whether your beliefs, habits or choices are useful. Are your beliefs, habits or choices empowering or disempowering you every day? Is it possible that one of your beliefs about money might be causing problems? If your beliefs lead to problems, then they are no longer useful to you. Replace them with those that are. Understanding this key point is important in developing new habits that serve you better and help to prevent problems in the future. For example, if you believe that it is hard to get out of debt, simply imagine that it is easy. Make the picture of yourself doing this just as real as possible and experience the positive feelings you get as you live out this new belief. Act as if it were easy to get out of debt by taking one small action each day to remind yourself of your new belief.

CHOICE CREATES EMPOWERMENT

You empower yourself with choices. Rigid beliefs rob people of their power of choice, keep them stuck in old habits and are disempowering. Rigid beliefs disempower individuals and institutions alike by causing them to stop searching for new choices and new solutions. Flexible beliefs create choices. In other words, we empower ourselves with flexible beliefs.

Watch out for beliefs about yourself and money that you are sure about. Certainty can keep people stuck with ineffective ways of thinking and dealing with problems. The problems to deal with are not the financial circumstances people confront but how they interpret and respond to those circumstances. In other words, your attitudes and beliefs about a financial problem are really the problem, because they determine what responses you will make. Practice the art of not knowing; pretend for a few days that your mind is a blank slate. By doing so, you will be open to a new range of possibilities.

Another common reason why many people never become financially secure is that they think financial matters are too complex. They want to turn over the responsibility for controlling their own financial lives to an expert. It's like going to see a marriage counselor and asking her to take responsibility for your marriage or asking a therapist to take responsibility for your own emotional well-being. If you exclusively depend on someone else, you'll always have someone else to blame for what happens. However, with control of your financial life you conquer one of life's most important areas. By doing so, you increase your personal confidence and your self-esteem enormously. You begin to think that if you can control your money (something you thought you could not do), then you can control everything else in your life as well. You find that gaining control of your financial life leads to increased confidence and self-esteem. That control symbolizes personal growth and greater freedom. As you gain financial control in your life, keep in mind three things:

First, you need to become clear about all the things you can do for yourself and your family and the peace of mind you'll feel when you have greater financial control. Financial success begins in your mind. You need to see it in your mind before you'll see it in your life. Whatever you focus on will grow and become your reality. If you do not like what you're seeing, then change the channel. Change what you're watching, what you're focusing on, and you will begin empowering yourself and finding answers to your financial problems much more easily.

Second, *mindfulness* rather than *mindlessness* means anticipating and planning your actions rather than just reacting to daily crises. It also means paying attention to what you are doing rather than worrying about what you've done afterwards. This results in a purposeful use of money rather than a haphazard use of it. Pointless spending results in continually missing your mark in life. You sacrifice what you really need and want, for things that do not really matter to you later.

Third, ask yourself if someone were to offer you a trip with no destination, no road map, no compass and not even a spare tire in the car, would you go? People without financial goals and plans are like someone on just such a trip, and savings is the spare they lack when a tire eventually goes flat. Goals and plans guide you in every financial decision you make and are like a map and compass to help make sure that you do not take the wrong road. Financial goals and plans give you a sense of control, direction, progress, stability and most of all, freedom and peace of mind. Goals and plans help ensure that you use your money for what is most important to you.

Those people who claim that they were doing okay financially until some unexpected or unpredicted emergency arose are usually not doing nearly as well as they think. Financial emergencies are an in-evitable reality. If you do not anticipate and prepare in advance for financial emergencies, you'll live from crisis to crisis. You'll scramble to cope with each crisis as it occurs, then worry about when the next one might occur. Freedom and peace of mind under such circumstances are impossible.

TAKING CHARGE OF YOUR FINANCES

Develop one or more financial goals and a spending plan. You will then find that your finances and your entire life have a much better balance and focus. Carelessness with money, such as spending it as fast as you make it, using charge cards recklessly and having no savings for emergencies suggests that your financial life is out of balance. This causes other aspects of your life to get out of balance as well. As you plan, you can still live in the present if you do the following:

- Track your expenses.
- Have a written spending plan.
- Reduce your dependence on credit cards and other credit.
- Pay off the entire balance of your credit cards each month.
- Save some money each pay period.
- Balance your checkbook.

These tasks will help you regain a sense of balance and stability in your life. They will give your life some structure and sense of security and build your confidence and self-esteem. These tasks are particularly important if you are currently recovering from a difficult period in your life such as separation, divorce, widowhood, unemployment or substance abuse. Doing these tasks, you will lose your fear of money and gain more confidence in money matters. You will find it easier to gain a clearer sense of direction in other areas of your life as well.

These tasks also help you to develop a much clearer focus. Focus simply means that your money will flow in whatever direction you choose and into whatever receptacle you create for it. If you have always operated on a survival level, meeting basic needs, then that is where your money will always go, even with more of it. Without a written spending plan, your financial life will quickly get out of focus. There may never be enough money left over for things that are really important to you. Every time you get additional money, there will always be some unmet basic need or responsibility where it must go, and you will end up feeling out of control.

You can find many books and seminars today on strategies for managing your money or how to accumulate wealth. However, you will never improve your financial life simply by reading a book or attending a seminar, regardless of how good the book or seminar is. Your own common sense tells you that expecting your life to improve by reading a book or attending a seminar is like expecting to learn to drive a car just by reading a book or attending a seminar. At some point you have to get behind the wheel in order to learn to drive, don't you? Improving your financial life is no different. It requires you to actually do something with the information provided here.

Throughout this book there are places for you to interact with the information by asking yourself questions, and other places to write down your own ideas on how certain information relates to you, your life and your beliefs. The Money Mastery plan provided at the end of this book works. It has worked for my financial counseling clients for many years, and it absolutely will work for you provided that you involve yourself fully. The plan doesn't require a lot of time, but it does require a few minutes a day done consistently every day for an extended period of time. This is a small price to pay for financial security and peace of mind, greater control over your life, and greater self-confidence and self-esteem.

2.

LEARNING TO ACHIEVE YOUR FINANCIAL GOALS

You can find lots of information about setting goals and making New Year's resolutions. However, you will find almost nothing on why resolutions are so rarely kept and goals so often abandoned. A 1993 Gallup poll showed that 48 percent of the people interviewed had made New Year's resolutions. This included 22 percent who resolved to get control of their personal finances. Of the 48 percent, over half (52%) admitted that they did not keep their resolutions, saying that they lacked willpower (42%), lost interest (29%) or had unreachable goals (17%). Another study showed that four out of five people who make New Year's resolutions to lose weight have given up by the end of April, and less than one in ten people (9%) will actually keep their resolutions.

WHY PEOPLE DON'T ACHIEVE THEIR GOALS

Why do so many people believe that keeping resolutions and achieving goals is hard? Keeping resolutions or achieving goals has little to do with willpower, seriousness or whether goals are unreachable. Resolutions and goals are conscious intentions to make decisive changes in personal habits. However, personal habits are usually habitual responses made without conscious awareness. These automatic and subconscious responses are determined by life experiences, values and beliefs.

The reason why willpower usually fails is because it is a function of your conscious mind. Trying to use conscious willpower to change subconscious habits is nearly always futile. Instead of trying to use willpower to gain control of your life, let your imagination guide you.

For example, Jane Abbott, a 32-year-old social worker, came to me because she had problems reaching her financial goal to save enough money for a down payment on a house. She said, "For some reason that I don't understand, I'm earning enough money, but I just can't seem to save any. The strange thing is that all of my coworkers and friends say that I am a very disciplined person in other areas of my life. Why don't I have enough willpower to save a little money?" When describing to me how she had been trying to save money, she spoke about willpower, saying that she denied herself certain purchases she wanted and turned down invitations to events that she wanted to attend. There are many people who diet in the same way, but if they try to lose weight by depriving themselves of the food they want and that their bodies need, they are doomed to fail in the long run. Similarly, people who attempt to save money based on deprivation and willpower also are doomed to failure.

I simply asked her, "Tell me what is so important about buying a house?" She then spent the next several minutes describing what it meant for her self-esteem, self-respect, her independence and sense of accomplishment. I then asked her to list the activities she saw herself doing. After she described the many activities she would enjoy both inside and outside the house, I asked her to clip a photo of a house she thought was attractive from a magazine or newspaper and make two extra copies of it. I had her tape one copy to her bathroom mirror, another to the refrigerator and the third inside her checkbook. I then asked her to take three moments each day to visualize herself in her house doing things she enjoyed and hear her voice as well as the voices of other people as she visualized these pictures. Finally, we developed a spending and saving plan based in large part on that powerful, ever-present picture of her inside her house. Within a year she had accumulated enough for a down payment. Eighteen months later she called to invite me to her housewarming party.

When we are unsuccessful in using willpower to achieve goals and resolutions, we often judge or condemn our efforts and label ourselves as failures. We then try to find conscious answers for having failed to change subconscious habits. This wasted effort leads to frustration and self-criticism and to making excuses for having slipped. Such self-criticism damages our self-esteem. It is nearly impossible to accomplish goals or keep resolutions if you criticize yourself or draw negative conclusions about yourself and your efforts. This is why people assume that keeping resolutions, reaching goals and making changes in their lives take a long time and must be difficult.

OTHER REASONS WHY PEOPLE GIVE UP

How you feel about yourself and your ability to succeed can affect your success in achieving your goals in other ways, as well. If you find yourself blocked, then either your vision of yourself having already accomplished your goal is unclear, or you are disabling rather than enabling yourself with your self-talk. What you are seeing in your mind and how you are talking to yourself about your goal will determine whether or not you succeed. Such disabling mental pictures and self-talk result from internal conflicts about your goals, a feeling of needing permission from someone to succeed, not breaking goals down into small simple steps so that you can actually see these steps clearly in your mind, or focusing on times when you haven't achieved a goal.

Conflicts about your goals. It is nearly impossible to achieve your goals if you

- aren't sure of their importance;
- don't believe you deserve them;
- don't really believe you can achieve them; or
- have goals that conflict with each other.

When talking about your goals, look for phrases that may indicate conflicts, usually involving such words as *but, although, however,* or statements such as "I'd really like to have this, but I don't have time to pursue it right now." "Part of me wants this, but on the other hand . . ." "Although I could have this goal if I wanted to, at the same time, I need to do something else first." "I'd like to save money, but I'm afraid it would restrict me too much." "I could save money for a house; however, it would mean depriving myself." Such phrases are clues that you may have to resolve some self-determined barriers that are keeping you from reaching your goals.

Needing permission to succeed. If you find yourself unintentionally sabotaging your own efforts, such self-sabotaging behavior often results from prior conditioning by parents or others who made you feel unworthy or incompetent. If so, you need to ask yourself an important question: "*Whose* permission do I need before I can achieve this goal? Is someone's permission necessary to achieve this goal?" If the answer to this question is "Yes, someone's permission is needed," then *you* need to give yourself permission. Speak to yourself in the second person as if you were someone else; for example, "Mary, your goal is worthwhile, and you have my permission to succeed!"

Focusing on times when you haven't achieved a goal, instead of times when you have been successful. This thinking causes you to get entangled in seeking conscious explanations for subconscious failure as explained earlier. You need to approach your goals as if you have already accomplished them. By focusing on times when you have been successful, you empower yourself because you are able to see what you were doing, how you organized the task, and what you were thinking, feeling and saying to motivate yourself that enabled you to succeed. Then see yourself doing the same thing and talking to yourself in the same way as you approach your new goal. Change your mental pictures and change the way you talk to yourself about your goal, and you will ensure a successful outcome.

How Goals Are Actually Achieved

Goals can be described as "dreams with a due date." To achieve your goal, substitute imagination for willpower. Imagine a motion picture of your life with you having already achieved your goal. If you cannot see it in your mind, you won't see it in your life. Achieving goals starts with imagining yourself having already accomplished the change you want. If this doesn't inspire you, then imagine the opposite for a moment. What will your life continue to be like if you don't achieve your goal, if you don't change what you have been doing? What will it cost you in terms of money, relationships, career success and peace of mind? If you continue to do what you've been doing, you'll continue to get what you've been getting. Is this how you choose to spend the rest of your life? A definition of insanity is "continuing to do the same thing over and over again and expecting different results." The word *resolutions (re-solutions)* implies a commitment to new solutions, a commitment to doing things differently.

To change your life for the better, you must first change your attitude, and before you can change your attitude, you must change your beliefs. For example, let's say you want to change because you now believe that you and your loved ones deserve a better life. No financial improvement in your life can occur until you want it so much that you are willing to change your attitudes and your beliefs to make it happen. Sometimes people aren't fully experiencing the pain or other consequences of what they're doing yet or aren't aware that what they've been doing isn't working, that they need to do something differently. Sometimes people are more interested in whether their financial beliefs are right than if the beliefs are no longer useful and prevent them from having a better life.

Your mental images, the way you talk to yourself about your goal and your efforts to achieve that goal, will make change easier for you. How effective you will be is determined by the feeling you get when you focus on having already achieved your goal. People are much more motivated to act not by what they know, but by how they *feel* about what they know.

HOW A WELL-DEFINED GOAL IS STATED

A goal that is too broadly defined, with no particular thought as to whether or not it is achievable, realistic or positive, usually will not succeed. Check your goal with the following criteria. If your goal meets these important criteria, you are already one-third of the way toward achieving it.

State your goal in a positive manner. Determine what you want, not what you don't want. When you focus your attention on what you don't want, you program yourself to do the very thing you want to avoid or to change. If you find yourself stating a goal in terms of what you no longer want in your life or what you wish to avoid, then ask yourself, "What will I be doing instead?" Write down your answer. Imagine what you will be seeing, what you'll be hearing and what you'll be feeling when you have already achieved the goal. Make this visualization a part of your daily routine.

State your goal as if it were already happening. What will you be doing and how will you be doing it? Use the gerund or *-ing* ending on the verbs you use to state your goal, such as "I will be *saving* $10 a month for emergencies." Stating your goal in this way establishes action and momentum.

Only write about what you can do right now. Goal setting without action is only wishful thinking. You don't need to do it perfectly; you only need to begin by taking a small step now. Waiting for the perfect time or place or for circumstances to improve leads to endless procrastination and is an excuse not to begin.

Make your goal as specific as possible. How exactly are you going to accomplish this goal? For example, instead of writing "I'm going to save money for my vacation," you should write, "I'll have $120 saved for a vacation this year by saving $10 per paycheck." Instead of writing, "I want to feel better about myself so I won't spend money," you should write, "I'm going for a walk when I get depressed or lonely instead of spending money." Note that the phrase "I want to feel better about myself" is wishful thinking, not a goal. A goal specifically states what you can do and say to make yourself feel better.

Break your goals down into small steps. Doing so makes them more doable and allows some early signs of success. Achieving the smaller goals you set for yourself will gradually give you the confidence to attain your ambitions on a larger scale.

State your goal only in terms of what you can control. Your goal cannot depend on what other people may or may not do or on other events taking place. Statements such as "I want my wife to be more responsible with money" or "I want my ex-husband to meet his financial responsibilities before I . . ." are not acceptable goals since the actions of others are not in your control.

HOW TO ACHIEVE YOUR GOALS

Stating your goal properly is the first part of goal success. You then need to combine a well-defined goal with other steps to make certain that your goal becomes a reality.

Know what you really want. We need to ask ourselves, "What is the goal of the goal? What will it do for me that's positive?" For example, if your goal is to get a certain job, this could be a way for you to achieve many other important goals such as to become more creative, have more on-the-job freedom or more financial independence. Your real goal is not that particular job but the positive things it will do for you.

If your goal is to have more money, ask yourself, "What will having more money do for me that's positive?" Then use your answer to ask again, "So, what will having that (your previous answer) do for me?" Asking yourself this question several times lets you discover the real or key goal that's most important to you. Once you know your key goal, then you are more flexible, more motivated and have more options to attain it. When you know what you really want and why, you're much more likely to get it.

Expect to succeed and believe that changes are possible, that you can and will make these changes happen. Put a picture of your financial goal (preferably in color) from a magazine or newspaper on a bathroom or bedroom mirror as a constant reminder.

Three times a day, mentally rehearse and enjoy the experience of achieving your goal. See, feel and hear yourself living as if your goal is already achieved. Act as if your desired change has already occurred. Then from this vantage point, look back at yourself making the decision and starting the process. As you mentally rehearse the experience of achieving your goal, encourage yourself by talking to yourself in this way: "You want to, you can, you've already started, you are now (your goal)." Then do it in the first person: "I want to, I can, I've already started, I am now (your goal)." Do this three times a day.

Recall and relive previous successful experiences. What is the most important goal you have ever achieved? As you relive that experience, ask yourself these questions: "What was the first thing I thought about and saw in my mind to motivate myself?" "How did I feel and what did I say to myself after completing each step along the way?" "How did I feel and what did I say to myself when I had actually achieved my goal?"

Keep a daily journal. Keeping a daily journal helps you to understand more fully and to integrate into your behavior what you are experiencing. In your journal, focus on what in your life is working and what you would like to continue. As you do this, you will also notice other things that may not be working for you that you do not want to continue.

Be curious, not judgmental. See unsuccessful attempts only as results and not as failure. Use these results as information or feedback to modify what you've been doing. Be flexible; modify your goal or the time desired to achieve it if your circumstances change.

Reward yourself when you have made some progress. Do so after completing each step along the way rather than waiting until you have fully achieved your goal. Enjoy and congratulate yourself after completing each step. Most people say something like, "There, that's done; what's next?" What do you usually say to yourself when you have just completed a step or part of an important task?

Achieving your financial goals themselves will never make you happy in the long run; it's who you become, as you overcome the obstacles necessary to achieve your goals, that will give you the deepest and most long-lasting sense of fulfillment. Even if, for some reason, you don't achieve your goal, take heart, because the process itself of working consistently toward your goal, will empower you and produce positive changes and positive habits!

EMPOWERING BELIEFS AND SELF-TALK

You reflect your self-confidence and belief in yourself by the language of your self-talk. Your self-talk can empower you and get you unstuck and moving. Or, if you allow it, it can disable you and keep you stuck. It can reinforce any negative beliefs you might have about yourself and about your lack of financial control. When you change your self-talk, you change the meaning of your experiences. For example, read each of the following statements aloud. After each sentence, picture yourself in relation to the tasks that are mentioned. Are you seeing the experience on a screen or as if you were there? Notice how much different the reality and immediacy of each of these stated actions feels.

I dance.	I danced.
I'm going dancing.	I was dancing.
I will dance.	I've gone dancing.
I will be dancing.	I used to go dancing.

Verb tense can have an enormous effect on how we feel about a problem. Notice the difference in how you feel about your problem as you say the following sentences to yourself: "It is a problem, isn't it?" Now, say to yourself, "That has been a problem, hasn't it?" Then say to yourself, "That used to be a problem, didn't it?"

Do you see the difference in how you feel just by the way you talk to yourself? Which sentence makes you feel more powerful and positive? Which sentence makes you feel the least powerful and positive?

Although the past cannot be changed, we can change our present memories and interpretations of the past. Begin thinking of current problems as in the process of being solved by learning to think and speak of them in the past tense. For example, if someone says, "I always run short of money by the end of the month. Managing my money is a problem," he is making a generalization and framing his problem as if expecting the problem to continue forever.

Instead, it is more empowering to say to yourself, "So, this has been a problem. Every month I have found myself running out of money by the end of the month." With this powerful change in verb tense you are telling yourself that the problem is soon to be in the past. Then you can begin to direct your thinking toward what you want in the future by saying something like, "And I'm now making things different." Stating a problem in the past tense makes a profound difference in how you regard it and in your confidence level as you take steps to resolve it.

Also, when using self-talk it will help you to become more successful in changing your behavior by stating your goals as if you are in the process of accomplishing them. As you answer these questions, look up at the ceiling and pay close attention to your mental images and feelings:

- "What resources do I have that will enable me to gain control of my spending more easily?"

- "What will be my first indication that I already have better control of my money?"

- "Will I have a feeling of accomplishment and terrific self-esteem once I have paid off all my credit cards, or even when I have made some progress in doing so?"

- "Will it be after the first or second month of following my written spending plan that I will find it strange my finances could ever have been in such bad shape?"

Once you begin to think of your desired outcome as something that is inevitable, it's easier to do what's necessary to make it happen. Here are some additional examples:

- "How will I be managing my money differently when I am managing it in a way that is fully satisfying to me?"

- "When will I first notice that saving money has helped me to have even more of what I want, not less?"

- "I wonder how long after my spouse and I have begun saving for retirement will we both realize that it has made us more secure and confident about our financial life?"

Now it's your turn! Using the examples given above, take something in your financial life that you want to change, and state it as if it is in the process of happening right now.

_____

_____

_____

_____

_____

CONDITIONAL OR NEGATIVE LANGUAGE

Another important principle to keep in mind is not to get stuck in conditional or negative language. Conditional language uses the word *would* as in "If I thought it would do any good, I would contact this creditor right away." (This is called being lost in the "woulds.") Negative language is any language that uses a negative modifier, such as "don't want to incur any more debt." Remember that everything you say is being stored in your subconscious. In saying the previous sentence, your mind is probably going to focus more on the word *debt* than on the words *don't want*. Instead, frame everything you do using positive action words. Action words and phrases that are likely to lead to positive results include: "I want to . . . , I can, I am, I choose to, I get to, I'm determined to, let's." Imagine what you will be doing as if it is already happening, and talk to yourself in the same way.

QUESTIONS PROVIDE SOLUTIONS

The questions that you ask yourself provide solutions to your financial problems. These questions can get your financial life back on track because they direct your attention and how you think, feel and respond to your problem. Your questions contain assumptions, reflect your beliefs about yourself and money, and are highly suggestive. These questions can empower you, set a new direction and give you the confidence to take the necessary steps in the right direction. The three most important questions to ask yourself are:

1. "What is my goal?"

2. "What am I doing that's working now?"

3. "How do I manage to do that? (How do I make that happen?)"

"What is my goal?" focuses your attention on the outcome you want rather than on the problem. Yet most people respond to this question by describing what they do not want or what they want someone else to do. Therefore, it is important to get yourself to describe what you will be doing differently when you get your financial life in order. This includes describing what you will be saying to yourself and how you will be feeling when you achieve your goal. You may find that your answer to this question alone may be all that is necessary to accomplish your goal.

If you respond negatively to this goal question, in terms of what you do not want, then ask yourself, "So I don't want to . . . ; What do I want instead?" For example, if you say, "I don't want to constantly run out of money before the end of the month," ask yourself, "What do I see myself doing instead to keep this from happening?" Notice that this question causes you to construct a mental movie of yourself doing what needs to be done. If you cannot see yourself in your mind doing what needs to be done, you will not see it in your life. Become the star in your movie. After all, it's your movie, and if you can see what you want in your movie, then you can see it in your life.

If you find yourself responding to this goal question with very vague ideas, then use the following questions to help you define your goal more clearly:

- "How will I know when I am in control of my financial situation?"

- "What am I doing differently during these times when I am in control of my financial situation?"

- "How will I know that I'm making progress with this?"

- "What will I be doing? How will I talk to myself as I complete each step?"

- "How will I talk to my husband/wife? What tone of voice will I use with myself and with my husband/wife?"

- "How will I handle my bills differently?"

- "How will I use my credit cards differently?"

- "What else do I see myself doing differently?"

If you say to yourself, "Most of the time I don't do (whatever it is that is causing problems)," this implies that there are certain times when you are handling money in ways that do not cause problems. Therefore, ask yourself:

- "How are those times when I'm handling money the way I want different from those other times when I'm not?"

- "What am I saying to myself then?"

- "In what situations am I doing this?"

- "How did I manage to do this then?" or "How did I *decide* to do this then?"

I've shown you a few foolproof techniques for achieving your financial goals. By stating your goals in ways that are positive and that meet the other important criteria, you are a third of the way to accomplishing them. Regularly visualizing yourself as if you have already achieved them and talking to yourself as if they were already in the process of being achieved, empowers you to take action and gets you two-thirds of the way there. The last third simply requires that you take action. Short, simple and consistent action will lead to inevitable achievement of your financial goals.

3.

OVERCOMING BELIEFS
THAT LIMIT SUCCESS

SELF-LIMITING BELIEFS ABOUT YOURSELF
AND MONEY

Self-limiting beliefs about yourself and money result when you distort
or delete parts of your experiences or make faulty generalizations
from your experiences. Distortions result from misinterpreting your
experiences. Deletions result from omitting aspects of your experience. Generalizations result from forming inappropriate opinions or
beliefs about life from a specific event. For example, a friend of mine
made a bad serve in tennis. She was upset and began a sequence of
self-talk statements by drawing inappropriate generalizations such as:

- "Gee, that was a bad serve." (leading to . . .)
- "I never could serve very well." (leading to . . .)
- "When I think about it, all of my shots are bad." (leading to . . .)
- "In fact, I'm really not a very good tennis player." (leading to . . .)
- "I'd better face the fact that I'm not much good at sports at all." (leading to . . .)
- "I'd better accept the fact that I'm an awkward klutz; there's not much of anything that I can do without fouling up somehow."

In other words, from just one bad tennis serve she began talking to
herself negatively. She internalized this one action as a negative belief
about herself as a human being. People often do this to themselves
with financial problems. Such self-limiting beliefs and negative self-talk

will cause continued financial problems until people become aware of what they are doing and substitute more empowering language.

People often say or imply, "I want to get rid of this problem, but I don't want to change anything I'm doing." Some people think that admitting a need to change is the same as admitting that they are not good enough the way they are, that they have somehow failed. The need to change threatens some people's self-esteem, so they defend their behavior to protect themselves from feelings of worthlessness or inadequacy. How often have you heard the cliché, "Change is hard"? As a result, people learn to associate change with difficulty and with a high prospect of failure. Then they react by backing off from anything that implies that they might fail.

Such an attitude can be an obstacle to efforts to gain better financial control of your life by changing what you are doing. However, changing is often easier and less painful than what you're currently experiencing. Also, changing what you've been doing is essential to resolve any problems and to prevent similar problems from occurring in the future. There are four fundamental principles to remember with respect to changing money management beliefs and habits:

1. You can only change yourself. You cannot change other people, and this includes your husband or wife's beliefs and habits with money.

2. You will change when you become aware of what is not working, or when the negative consequences from what you are doing become bad enough.

3. You can choose to change what you are doing that is contributing to your financial problems, or choose to live with those financial problems for the rest of your life.

4. You will choose the most useful response once you discover that you really do have a choice. Always make decisions that open up and move you in the direction of more choices.

Most people think that personal change is difficult or takes a long time. They have tried repeatedly through willpower to make changes, and it has not worked. They then assume that personal change takes a long time and must be hard. Willpower by itself is not enough, however. If we can create problems in a moment, then we can create solutions in a moment too, if we believe that we can and must do it. You can do this in just three key steps.

1. See the change in your mind as if it has already happened.

2. Say to yourself, "I must change this situation; I can change it, and I am changing it *now*." In other words, whenever you hear yourself saying, "I can't," then say to yourself, "therefore, I must!"

3. Begin acting as if the change has already begun to happen.

FEELING CONFUSED OR STUCK

Jim and Mary Swenson were referred to me by another financial counselor who had been having trouble helping the couple. In trying to help them unravel their financial problems, the counselor found that the couple became more and more confused and stuck as the session progressed.

When they entered my office they were very pessimistic about getting their financial lives in order, and while shaking their heads, mentioned that they would most likely end up filing for bankruptcy. I noticed that as they began describing their financial situation, like so many other clients, they tended to stack their financial problems on top of each other so that they weren't able to deal with one problem at a time but were mixing all of their financial problems together. I also noticed several other things: First, they were able to come up with several very positive steps that would have improved their financial situation, but they tended to disparage or discard their own ideas just as fast as they were able to think of them. Stacking or lumping problems together—financial and other problems—is typical of people who are feeling overwhelmed. Second, their body language and the way they spoke about their problems was highly revealing. Both of them sat slumped in their chairs. Their heads were down, eyes were glued to the floor, and their heads swung back and forth from left to right as they spoke. The more they spoke, the deeper their frowns became, and their breathing, which was irregular and shallow to begin with, became even more so. Looking down at the floor to his right, Mr. Swenson said, "We're downright stuck!"

No wonder they were stuck. Before we did anything about their problems, I first had to interrupt their stuck feelings and their mental rehearsal of all their problems. These highly charged and negative feelings were preventing them from seeing any solutions or even talking objectively about their problems. I did this by asking them to sit back in their chairs, put their shoulders back and look up at the ceiling. Then, I asked them to take just a moment or two to breathe deeply with me. After a minute or two, their normal breathing was restored. At about that time, their heads and eyes started to look down at the floor again. I stood up and made eye contact with them, forcing their eyes up from the floor to meet mine. Then I sat back down. Every time they began to look back down at the floor, I would start to get up, and their heads and eyes would come up to meet mine.

After restoring their breathing and calming them down, I then had them imagine that they were sitting in the projection booth of a movie theater with a movie projector at their side, watching themselves in a movie of their financial problems. When I noticed them beginning to frown and become panicky with the scenes of the movie, I then asked them to run the movie as a series of slides, one at a time, stop the projector at any time they wanted while watching any slide and comment on what was happening. As they did this, they discovered that they were leaving out certain slides about these events, and that other slides were out of place and needed to be moved around. After making these adjustments to this slide show of events, I asked them to imagine putting frames around each slide, until the slide looked quite different. We played with their slide show for about twenty minutes. During this time, I watched their faces closely as they began to see all kinds of new things about specific events and circumstances of their financial problems, that they had not been aware of. As they stopped the slide show from time to time, moved the sequence of slides around and added a slide or two here and there, they developed a totally new perspective on their financial problems. The looks on their faces were priceless, as occasionally one of them would say something like, "Well, I'll be darned; I forgot about that," or "Gee, I hadn't thought about that." After unstacking their problems this way, we developed a specific plan to deal with them one at a time, giving Mr. Swenson the responsibility for certain problems and Mrs. Swenson responsibility for other problems.

People are always clearer about their problems than about possible solutions. They have been living with and worrying about their problems day and night, but cannot imagine what life could be like without the problems. Whenever you're feeling confused, take comfort because being confused is probably the best thing that could happen to you. Confusion is a pathway to understanding. Being confused is so scary and uncomfortable for most people that they will do whatever is necessary, right away, just to end it. Being confused usually means that you have enough information, but that you simply have not organized it yet in a way that makes sense. When you are feeling confused, simply ask yourself, "What exactly am I confused about?" "At what point did I become confused?"

Notice that whenever you feel stuck, you tend to use the word *just* in describing your situation. The word *just* discounts everything else about a situation, justifying and continuing negative feelings and behavior instead of trying out new feelings and behavior. The key word *just* tells you when or how you became stuck in an attitude, behavior or feeling, and what must be done to help you. For example, "It's just the way it is." "I can't help it; it's just the way I feel about it." "Saving money is just something I can't do." When you hear yourself using the word *just,* you have handcuffed yourself to what you have been doing that is no longer working for you.

If you feel confused, it's often because you may have a series of images in your head in a chaotic jumble. On the other hand, if you get confused when things are described too slowly and in too much detail, you need to see these images like a movie, to see how things relate to each other; otherwise, the process is too disconnected for you to make sense of it.

If you feel stuck or confused, notice that your breathing may have become irregular and shallow. Since irregular or shallow breathing often accompanies being stuck or confused, simply sit in a chair with your shoulders back and head upright and breathe normally for a few moments. This will often eliminate your feeling of being stuck or confused, or at least help you more rapidly become unstuck.

If you feel stuck or confused, most likely you have a picture of yourself mired in concrete, stuck to flypaper or glue, in handcuffs, leg shackles or a straightjacket. These pictures are also likely to be in black and white (as opposed to color), dim, out of focus, unclear and have no movement or sound.

You can quickly get out of this state of mind simply by bringing this stuck picture of yourself into focus. Add color, movement and sounds (voices or even music) to it. As you do so, pay close attention to what happens. Ask yourself questions that make you visualize yourself in that situation with movement, color and sounds. Then speed up both the movement and the sounds connected with your picture. This simple empowering visualization exercise will help you to see things from a new perspective, to begin making decisions and taking action. It may help in doing this to imagine yourself sitting in the projection booth of a movie theater with the movie projector at your side, watching a movie of yourself in your confused or stuck situation. As you do, play the movie in slow motion. Then run the movie in reverse (play it backwards). In doing so, you may discover exactly at what point you get confused, and exactly what has confused you. Play it again as if it were a series of slides that you can show one at a time. As you watch the movie or slide show you may find that you have left out a step, or that two steps are out of sequence and need switching. As you do this, notice how quickly the confusion stops.

FEELING VICTIMIZED

Tina Edmondson, the divorced mother of a 15-year-old daughter, came to me for financial counseling. As she described her financial problems, she repeatedly referred to her ex-husband as an irresponsible person who owed her nearly $3,500 in child support payments, and said if only he could be made to meet his responsibilities, her financial problems and a lot of other related problems would be solved. Tina's problem in collecting child support may well be a common problem today, but she had been responding to it over and over again in the same totally unproductive way.

I reviewed with her what action she had already taken about her financial problems, and she responded with what action she had taken repeatedly to find her ex-husband and to get him to meet his child support responsibilities. In other words, other than fixating on her irresponsible ex-husband and repeatedly trying to find him and to get child support payments, she had not done very much. She remained stuck and felt thoroughly victimized and very angry. It was clear that she had already done everything possible to get this child support, but it hadn't worked. Yet, she was so fixated on this that it prevented her from focusing on what other steps to improving the financial life for her and her daughter might be possible.

I told her my definition of insanity and that if what she had been doing didn't make her crazy, it most certainly would keep her stuck and increasingly frustrated. After a long pause, she said quietly, "Yes, I guess this describes me pretty well!" I then asked her if she planned to continue to live her life this way and mentioned how unpleasant and even frightening this must be for her. After another long pause, she said, "You're right, it's about time that I put this behind me, and get on with my life." I said that this sounded like a good idea to me, and asked her what were the other options she had been thinking of lately. Together we began to construct other solutions to her problems, solutions that once she began to act on them, stopped her from dwelling on her problems and refocused her attention on her own power and personal development. Months later I got a call from her, and I said, "You don't sound like the same person." She replied strongly, "I'm not," and went on to describe all the activities she was now engaged in, how much control she had developed over her life in just a few months and how much more powerful she felt.

Some people see themselves as victims of their financial circumstances. They not only blame other people and events for their financial problems but also expect others to rescue them or bail them out of their financial problems. It is easy to get stuck in this way of thinking. People who see themselves as victims, as persons who have been wronged, or who believe that their problems are caused by events and circumstances outside their control, are least likely to take steps to improve their situations. Victims lack self-confidence and believe that since they are not responsible for their problems, nothing they do would make any difference.

If you find yourself thinking this way, you're going to remain stuck with your financial problems for a long time. Even if you somehow resolve a particular problem, another will soon replace it. It may be true that someone, an ex-husband, an ex-wife or a boss, victimized you and left you with a problem. Not taking action because of it will keep you stuck forever, and that is no way for anyone to live. If you continue to feel like a victim, you will remain a victim, continually feeling victimized by your circumstances and responding like a victim. To break this self-destructive attitude, you must decide to take back your power. That is the only way to take control of your financial life. You can do this by not blaming yourself or other people and events for your financial situation and by taking full responsibility for it.

When you focus on how you were victimized, you are not paying attention to what is going on around you right now. Therefore, you make yourself vulnerable to other mistakes or to being victimized again. Refocus your attention on the here-and-now, on events and situations around you. Pay attention to what you are doing right now before doing it. Also, find just one small step that you can take now that will greatly affect your problem, even if the action does not entirely resolve the problem. You will begin to feel more powerful and more in control by taking small steps to correct your situation. Pay attention to what happens when you do this.

Some people, particularly those who blame others for their problems, respond negatively or in self-defeating ways to "get even" or to "pay someone back." If you find yourself wanting to get even with someone, ask yourself these questions:

- "What will that act do to resolve my problem? (And using your answer to this question, continue to ask . . .)

- "And what will that do to resolve my problem? (And using your previous answer again, ask . . .)

- "And what will that do to resolve my problem?

After asking yourself these questions several times using your prior answer each time, you will quickly see that your intended action is not going to help you at all. It is most likely going to hurt you. Merely responding out of hurt, anger or frustration is not in your own best interest and will only make matters worse.

FEARING FAILURE

Joan Robinson had given up. For years, she wanted to start taking courses at a local community college. She had started college years ago, but she dropped out to get married, had two sons and then a few years later got divorced. Since then, the harsh realities of getting and keeping a good job and supporting her two sons without a college education confronted her over and over again. She had purchased several books over the years on how to budget, and from time to time would try to follow the instructions for budgeting given in those books, and hopefully allow herself to save a few dollars each month for her tuition. But some emergency always seemed to arise, usually something such as band uniforms or other expenses for one of her sons or for some unexpected household expense. She concluded that budgeting just wasn't her thing, saying, "I just can't do it; I never could, and never will be able to." Having said this, she would then feel like a failure and become depressed for not being able to afford to go back to school, get a better job and improve her family's financial circumstances. She had been repeating this same pattern again and again for years.

In counseling her, I first helped her to understand that she was not a failure in having a hard time budgeting. On the contrary, she was probably part of a majority rather than a unique case. Second, I had her stop referring to herself and to her attempts as failures. She hadn't failed; she simply found ways not to do it. As a matter of fact, when she told me the kinds of books she had read and the methods given for setting up and following a budget, I could see it was no wonder she had trouble. Most of these methods resemble something right out of Charles Dickens's *A Christmas Carol,* with poor Bob Cratchit sitting there with a quill pen, trying to balance a thick ledger and spending hours finding a missing penny. Unless people are accountants, it is no wonder they have trouble.

I asked her, "At what point did you have trouble in setting up a plan for spending?" She replied, "A plan for what?" I showed her that we were going to forget that the nasty "B (budget) word" even existed and begin thinking in terms of a spending plan. A spending plan is just that, a plan to ensure that money spent is for those things that mean most, rather than money dribbled away on things that aren't nearly as important. She said, "But that requires knowing what you want." I replied, "Yes, and being able to prioritize what you want. We call that having a goal or financial destination while on your financial journey through life. Instead of something hard or distasteful, I think you'll find it a 'trip,' if you'll forgive the pun." When she laughed, I said, "Good, and I want you to keep on laughing. In fact, make this process into a game rather than continuing to think of it as something like having a root canal." I also told her I wanted her to start paying attention to what she was doing at the time she was doing it and pause for a moment to think before acting.

Next, I had her develop a simple method for keeping track of her spending for one month. This reality check was intended to help her find leaks in her spending and it did. As a matter of fact, she found so many leaks that she bought herself a child's piggy bank and began depositing the money in it that she previously leaked away in unconscious spending. Within a month she noticed a difference and within several months exclaimed, "My God, I actually have some real money saved; this is enough for a course or two at the college."

A fear of failure sometimes causes people to reject an approach or to cease any further effort rather than to modify slightly what they are doing. For example, imagine yourself saying, "Oh, I've tried that budgeting thing several times, and it doesn't work for me." Simply ask yourself, "At what point in the budgeting process have I gotten stuck? Which part of it has given me the most trouble?" Here are other examples of empowering self-talk to get yourself unstuck:

- "If my spending has been a little out of control, then does this mean that I'm ready to do something about it?"

- "Because I am aware that I can't continue to live like this any longer, it makes me determined to change it."

- "Instead of constantly kicking myself for that mistake, I can now focus on taking action to see that it never happens again."

- "As I begin tracking my spending, I'm also noticing that I'm doing some things very well and want to continue them."

- "In paying off my debts, I'm noticing how much more money I seem to have each month."

REVERSING NEGATIVE BELIEFS

Simply reversing any negative beliefs about yourself and your circumstances will enable you to identify the evidence for a new belief. About 80 percent of the time, where you might have previously felt unable to deal with a situation or take action, reversing your thinking will lead to a shift in your beliefs or actions. For example, if you have a negative belief that you have to carry credit cards with you when shopping, simply say the reverse to yourself: "How has the opposite of that belief been true at certain times in my life?" "How is the opposite of what I thought more true than the old belief?" Or ask yourself, "What is the opposite of that for me?" This is a quick, simple way of changing a "can't do" into a "no problem!" Here are some more examples:

> **Negative belief:** "I am inadequate when it comes to handling money."
> **Reversal:** "Is it possible that what I have been perceiving as inadequate might be an inadequate view of myself?"

> **Negative belief:** "I have to be perfect."
> **Reversal:** "The only thing I can do perfectly is to allow myself to be imperfect."

> **Negative belief:** "I'm too old to change careers."
> **Reversal:** "In what ways does being older make it easier to change careers?"

> **Negative belief:** "I may lose a great opportunity if I say no to a salesperson."
> **Reversal:** "In what ways does saying no create even more opportunities for me in the future?"

> **Negative belief:** "Saying no to myself when shopping prevents me from getting the things I want."
> **Reversal:** "When shopping, in what ways can saying no to myself help me have even more things that I really want?"

REFRAMING NEGATIVE BELIEFS

Reframing means that you can break out of self-limiting attitudes by simply giving a different interpretation to current or past events in your life. It means looking at things differently, just as a different kind of frame can make a picture look better. The classic case of reframing is Tom Sawyer, forced to spend a tedious day whitewashing a fence, and fearing an even worse calamity—ridicule by the other boys. He responds to the boys' taunts with the question, "How often does a boy get the chance to whitewash a fence?" Soon, he is being paid by the boys for the chance to do the job. Notice that instead of saying to himself and to the other boys that he's *got* to whitewash the fence, he declares that he *gets* to whitewash the fence. This small change in just one word creates a large difference in meaning. Just as a different frame around a picture can change its appearance, a different "mental frame" around a mental image of a problem can change its appearance also. Here are five ways to reframe negative beliefs:

1. Reframe unsuccessful attempts by adopting a more useful belief that there is no failure, only results, if you're willing to observe what is happening. Teach yourself to see any positive aspects or at least your own positive intention of what you are doing. The more specific you can be, the better.

2. Find humor in the negative event or situation.

3. Compare the negative event or situation to something worse that could have happened.

4. Look for how the negative event or situation eventually led to a positive outcome, maybe by starting you on a different and better path.

5. Find positive meanings to a negative event or situation. It might have been difficult in some respect but provided something very positive, either then or later.

Exercise

Using the above suggestions about reversing or reframing negative beliefs, jot down in the space provided any belief reversals or belief reframes of one or more of the following self-limiting statements that most apply to you. For example:

You: "I tried to do it, but I failed. I just couldn't do it."

Reframe: "No, I didn't fail. I simply discovered a way not to do it."

1. I have to pay $4,000 more in income tax this year than last year.

2. My business gives me almost no time to myself. I work over 60 hours a week.

3. Every time I begin to succeed in something, I sabotage my own success.

4. I'm not getting help from anyone right now; I've never had any help.

5. I've tried finding a job through classified ads, but I can't find one.

6. It seems as though we just live from paycheck to paycheck, and never get ahead.

7. The only way I could reduce my living expenses has been to buy less expensive food and fix cheaper meals.

8. We've gotten ourselves in debt way over our heads.

9. We always seem to have more bills to pay than money to pay them.

10. I make more money than my neighbor, but he seems to have a lot more than I do.

_____

_____

_____

_____

_____

_____

_____

SELF-LIMITING LANGUAGE

Words that we attach to our experiences become part of our experiences. Words that we use to explain our problems can become problems themselves. They either magnify or minimize the effects and the difficulties of our problems. The self-talk language you use tells you whether you are going to carry out the tasks that you need to do for yourself.

Qualifiers. If you say, "I should," or "I want to, but," these words usually lead to inaction; you are not likely to do what you have said that you *should* do. For example "I should diet." "I should get more exercise." Similar well-meaning words and phrases leading to inaction are "ought to," "supposed to," "need to," "may," "might," "possibly," "try," "hope," "wish," "could" or "would."

Phrases such as "maybe I can," "I might," "I'll try," "I hope so," imply, "maybe I can't," "maybe not," "might not," "possibly not." When you use these phrases, it shows a negative mind-set that nearly always wins and provides a ready-made excuse. Instead, describe exactly what you plan to do and then see yourself going through each step, including seeing what you are doing once you have already succeeded.

Don't. When you tell yourself "don't," or not to do something, you have offered no alternatives. You have focused all of your attention on what you don't want to do any longer. Before you can do something, you must first be able to picture it in your mind. How can you picture what you aren't going to do? When you say, "don't," you focus your attention on and inadvertently program yourself to do the very thing you don't want to do. For example, a recent television antidrug campaign featured a person sniffing cocaine while a voice said, "Don't take drugs." Research later showed that it caused recovering drug addicts who saw the ad to purchase and use illegal drugs again.

Clichés. People use clichés as a substitute for seeking reliable information. Clichés reflect core beliefs that keep us stuck in thinking and actions that no longer work. One of the most harmful and frequently used clichés today is, "No pain, no gain." This cliché has absolutely no place in our self-talk. Human beings instinctively move away from pain. This highly damaging cliché unintentionally programs you to avoid changing what you are doing that is creating problems, simply because change has been associated with pain. Another variation of this is, "Change is hard." Repeating this cliché can result in a self-fulfilling prophecy, which intimidates people and undermines their confidence for fear that they might fail. Be careful about the language you use with yourself so that you do not unintentionally program yourself to avoid taking effective action. Instead, replace a cliché like this with the belief that change at times is easy but at other times even easier!

I can't. If you hear yourself saying, "I can't," then immediately say to yourself, "therefore, I must, and I must start now!"

Yes, but . . . If you find yourself in a "yes, but" game with yourself, you have fallen into the trap of making excuses. There is a part of you that really does not want to change or does not believe that changing the current situation is possible.

DEPRESSING SELF-TALK

People with financial problems sometimes become depressed or worried and engage in depressing or worrying self-talk. They replay each depressing or worrying episode in their heads repeatedly. Getting stuck in depressing self-talk prevents people from focusing on what is going on right now and from taking action.

First, stop describing yourself with the word *depression,* or any term that implies that you are abnormal or mentally ill. It is perfectly normal for you to be unhappy about financial problems, and the word *unhappy* is a more appropriate description. Normal people experience normal unhappiness about normal problems. However, if depression is chronic, or if it affects your health or ability to function, then see a therapist.

Then, refocus your attention on the exceptions to your problem, on whatever in your financial situation is working and on whatever you are doing successfully. Refocus your attention on what is going on in the present and take action to control these things. For example, if you are unhappy about your inability to pay all of your credit card and other bills on time, talk to yourself in the following manner:

- "It seems as if I've been unhappy when I haven't been able to pay all of my bills on time." Notice the change in tense from present to past, "have been unhappy." A restatement in the past tense helps you restore your feelings of normality. It helps these feelings of unhappiness become part of the past. Once you have begun to see such things as being in the past, you can develop a more positive attitude. You see that it is in your power to put such attitudes and problems behind you.

- "Are there times when I can pay all of my bills on time?" The statement refocuses your attention onto the exceptions to your problem, that is, when you are in control.

- "What occurs during these times? What am I doing when I can pay these bills on time?" These questions help you to identify specific attitudes and actions that enable you to do this successfully at these times.

- "Since I could pay my bills on time once before, what is preventing me from doing so now?" The question identifies any specific obstacle that might be standing in the way, while helping you build a mental bridge between the successful and unsuccessful times.

- "What do I need to do now to once again pay these bills on time?" The statement helps you to see yourself taking specific actions to remove any obstacle.

In my years as a financial counselor, I have discovered that one of the main reasons why people feel bogged down in financial matters and why they are unable to motivate themselves to take action is because of their self-limiting beliefs and manner of talking to themselves. In most cases, people have been wading in the murky swamp of such disempowering beliefs and negative self-talk for so long, that they are no longer aware of them or of their powerfully disabling effects.

So, take a few moments now to identify your own self-limiting comments using the following typical examples. Then, do the exercise that follows in order to eliminate any such self-limiting comments from your beliefs and self-talk, once and forever. Go for it!

PRACTICE EXAMPLES

Examples of typical self-limiting comments are listed below, followed by questions for you to answer to yourself. Pick a comment below (numbers 1 to 7) that you have found yourself using and ask yourself three questions from the suggestions given below each comment. As you do, pay close attention to any mental images, self-talk and feelings you get.

1. "I worry about money and my financial future."

- "Has there ever been a time in my life when I didn't worry about money and my financial future?"
- "When do I not worry about money and my financial future?"
- "What part of that problem has me worried the most?"
- "So what is it that I could do for myself now so that I'm worried less and less?"
- "Having worried about my money and financial future long enough, am I now going to find ways to end those worries?"
- "What would have to happen for that worry to stop?"
- "What do I need to do for this worry to stop now?"

2. "I procrastinate when making financial decisions or taking action."

- "What's important or valuable about making financial decisions for myself?"
- "So I've been putting those things off long enough, and now I'm ready to start."
- "What makes me want to start making financial decisions for myself now?"
- "What has stopped me from making financial decisions?"

3. "If I make these financial decisions, it will mean that by investing more of my money, I'll have less available to spend."

- "How is the opposite of that belief really more true?"
- "In what way might these financial decisions result in having more money to spend?"
- "Eventually I'll have more money available to spend. I'll also have more freedom, more peace of mind and more self-pride."

4. "I can't track my spending."

- "What's important or valuable about tracking my spending?"
- "How exactly has that become a problem?"
- "What has stopped me?"
- "What has not tracking my spending already cost me?"
- "What would happen if I did track my spending?"
- "What would life be like when I'm tracking my spending?"
- "If a miracle were to happen tonight, and that problem were solved when I awoke tomorrow morning, how would my life be different?"

5. "Planning my spending restricts me; it puts me in a financial straightjacket."

- "In what ways might a plan of my spending remove my financial straightjacket and give me even more freedom than before?"
- "How is the opposite of what I thought about planning my spending more true than that old belief?"
- "What do I need to begin planning my spending?"
- "When I am planning my spending, what will have changed to allow me to do it?"
- "When I have begun to plan my spending, will I notice all the new benefits I've derived from it?"
- "Just how surprised will I be when I begin to enjoy all the benefits I'm getting from tracking my spending?"

6. "Financial planning interferes with my natural spontaneity."

- "Does planning other things interfere with my spontaneity?"
- "Is it possible that in planning certain things, I may find that the more I plan ahead the more freedom I have?"
- "How does spontaneity necessarily keep me from planning ahead?"
- "Will thinking that prevent me from ever freeing myself from financial worry?"
- "Will thinking that prevent me from ever gaining financial security?"

- "Is my spontaneity more important than financial peace of mind?"

- "Can I imagine how planning my financial future could make me more spontaneous, not less?"

- "How can I begin to spontaneously plan my finances?"

7. "I often buy things I don't need or want because they are on sale."

- "Did I ever not buy something when I found a sale?"

- "How is that time different from the time when I buy things on sale?"

- "Is something on sale always a good bargain?"

- "Which is more important, buying something I need or buying it on sale?"

- "Are buying things at sales more important to me than having the things I want?"

- "When I have bought something and later found that I didn't need it or like it, how have I felt afterwards?"

- "Are there other things I can do at those times when I'm tempted?"

- "What else brings me as much pleasure as buying at sales?"

- "Do I keep a written list of things I need?"

Exercise

Now that you have practiced asking yourself empowering questions, select *one* or *two* of the statements below that most applies to you. Ask yourself the same kinds of questions. You may wish to jot down your questions in the space provided. Notice your mental images and the tone of the self-talk that you are using as you do this.

1. I am embarrassed (or feel guilty) about my financial life.

2. I argue about money with family members.

3. I'm afraid to really know about my financial condition.

4. I get upset when talking about money.

5. I am not responsible for my financial situation.

6. I feel that my spending is out of control.

7. I have trouble saving money.

8. I can't be financially stable right now.

9. I don't deserve financial success.

10. I can't get my financial life under control until my "ex" starts making child support payments.

11. Focusing on money and material things is materialistic and un-spiritual.

12. I live in the present when it comes to my finances and don't worry about the future.

13. If I succeed, failure must be next.

14. If I'm too financially successful, people won't like me.

15. I sometimes buy things I don't want or need, because I feel that I can't get them later if I don't get them now.

16. Someone will eventually rescue me from all of this.

17. I often pick up the check when out with my friends.

18. I sometimes buy gifts for other people even when I can't afford it.

19. Sometimes I don't even like the things I've bought after I've bought them.

20. Shopping is my favorite recreation.

21. I often hide purchases other than gifts from my family.

22. I sometimes spend money to make up for other things that are missing in my life.

23. I am a workaholic.

24. I work my tail off and still don't have anything to show for it.

25. I guess that I rely too much on my credit cards.

26. I have trouble saying no to salespersons.

_____

_____

_____

_____

_____

_____

_____

_____

_____

CHALLENGING SELF-LIMITATIONS

By asking yourself effective questions you can identify what has been keeping you stuck, identify possible choices and motivate yourself to take action. The questions that you ask yourself are highly suggestive, focus your attention and direct any action that you take. They can challenge your self-limitations and counterproductive beliefs and behavior. Effective questions are those very questions that you have needed to ask yourself for some time. Do not be concerned if you are unable to immediately answer some of these questions. This inability to answer means you may be more fully reexamining your own experience, beliefs or behavior regarding financial attitudes and habits. Answers will come to you in time, and the best questions are those that require some time for reflection.

The following questions are very powerful and challenging to use in helping you resolve problems because they help you overcome self-limitations and start the process of change. As you ask yourself these questions, pay close attention to any mental pictures, voices and feelings that arise. Notice which of the questions has particular significance for you. As you answer these questions, you may develop a vivid mental picture and/or voice and a powerful feeling. This reveals how unpleasant life will be if things continue as they have been and do not change. On the other hand, remember how much more pleasant life could be if things do change.

1. "What will happen if I don't change?"
2. "What will it cost me?"
3. "What won't happen if I change?"
4. "What will my life be like after I make those changes?"

Did you get a particularly vivid mental image and feeling for one of these questions? If so, then ask yourself that particular question again. Then ask yourself these two questions:

1. "What has stopped me in the past?"
2. "What would I need *to do* for that to no longer stop me?"

For example, if you hear yourself saying to yourself, "I can't get control of my financial life." Ask yourself these four questions. Pause for a few moments after each to give yourself time to answer:

1. "What will happen if I don't get control of my financial life?"
2. "What will it cost me if I don't?"
3. "What won't happen if I get my financial life under control?"
4. "What will my life be like after I get my financial life under control?"

Now, ask yourself again the question which evoked the most vivid image and powerful feelings, and again, ask these two questions:

1. "What has stopped me in the past?"
2. "What do I need *to do* for that to no longer stop me?"

The following questions are effective in challenging money-related self-limiting beliefs, without sounding judgmental or critical and without making yourself defensive. These challenges are very effective in changing beliefs and behavior that have contributed to your financial problems. They make you face the contradiction between what you say you want and what you are doing. They make you aware of your own beliefs and actions that may be causing problems or preventing achievement of your desired outcomes. These challenges result in action. Finally, this solution-focused question process opens options and choices. Choose one of the following nine self-limiting comments that most applies to you and use several of the new responses given below it.

1. When you hear yourself saying, "I can't, should, should not, must, have to, need to . . . " then immediately respond by using one or more of the following examples:

Self-limiting comment: "I can't do this task."

New response: "Then I must!" "What's stopping me?" "What would happen if I did?"

EXAMPLES OF SELF-LIMITING COMMENTS	NEW RESPONSES
• I can't find a job.	• What makes it impossible?
• It's impossible to do anything about it now.	• What stops me?
• It's impossible to get myself out of this.	• What prevents me?
• It's impossible to plan for my future.	• What has blocked me from doing so?
• I'm unable to save money.	• What would happen if I did?
• I should try to pay this off.	• Can I imagine (think of) a situation in which I could?
• I should not be so impulsive.	
• I guess I should try to do something about it.	
• I suppose that I should start soon.	

2. When you hear yourself saying, " . . . but, however, although . . . ," then immediately respond by using one or more of the following examples:

Self-limiting comment: "I want to get a job, but I can't leave the children alone."

New response: "What would happen if I left the children alone?" "What would I need to do to get a job?"

EXAMPLES OF SELF-LIMITING COMMENTS	**NEW RESPONSES**
• I want to find a better job, but all the good ones are taken.	• What makes it impossible?
	• What prevents me?
• I want to pay off my loan, but I can't stop using my credit card.	• What has blocked me from doing so?
• I would start saving for retirement, however, I just can't find time to work out a plan.	
• Can I think of a circumstance in which I could?	
• What would I need to do to make this happen?	

3. **When you hear yourself saying, "... all, every, everything, everybody, always, never, no one ...," then simply use the same generalized word as a question: "All? Everybody? Every time? Never? Nobody? Not even once?"**

Self-limiting comment: "I never could manage my money."

New response: "Never? Not even once?" "Could I think of just one time when I did manage it?"

EXAMPLES OF SELF-LIMITING COMMENTS	**NEW RESPONSES**
• I never could do that.	• Never? Not even once? Can I think of just one time when I did?
• Every time I attempt to do this, I foul up.	
• I always have trouble remembering these things.	• Always? Not even once when it didn't happen or wasn't this way?
• I have absolutely nothing to rely on.	• Nothing? There is absolutely nothing that I can think of ...?

EXAMPLES OF SELF-LIMITING COMMENTS (CONTINUED)	NEW RESPONSES
• I never have time for this.	• Nobody? Not even one person?
• Nobody really understands what I am going through right now.	• Everyone? Every person that I can think of . . . ?
• Everyone in that place is having financial trouble.	
• He always spends money without considering the consequences.	

4. **When you begin doubting yourself, or doubting whether a proposed action will be effective, use one or more of the following examples:**

Self-limiting comment: "I've tried that before, and it didn't work."

New response: "What exactly did I try?" or "At what point did I get stuck?"

EXAMPLES OF SELF-LIMITING COMMENTS	NEW RESPONSES
• I'll try.	• How exactly do I see myself trying?
• I just can't handle it.	• What is it exactly that I've had trouble handling?
• I don't know what to do.	• About what exactly?
• I have a problem with that.	• With what exactly?
• I just can't win, no matter what I do.	• What is it that I haven't done yet?
	• At what point did I get stuck?

5. When you hear yourself blaming other people or circumstances for what has happened, then immediately respond by using one or more of the following examples:

Self-limiting comment: "This is starting to cause problems."

New response: "How exactly has it caused problems?" or "What kinds of problems exactly has it caused?"

EXAMPLES OF SELF-LIMITING COMMENTS	NEW RESPONSES
• Trying to make ends meet is beginning to get to me.	• How specifically has it . . . ?
• This is really setting me back.	• In what way exactly have I . . . ?
• I am forced to do it this way.	
• My employer is responsible for this.	
• They just ignored me when I did this.	
• My spouse acts irresponsibly when it comes to money.	
• They act like they don't care one way or another.	

6. When you hear yourself accepting a bad situation as inevitable or out of your control, or as a reality rather than as something that you can change, then use these new responses:

Self-limiting comment: "Unfortunately, this problem is her fault."

New response: "This problem is unfortunate to whom exactly?"

EXAMPLES OF SELF-LIMITING COMMENTS	NEW RESPONSES
• This is clearly impossible.	• To whom exactly is it clear?
• This is obviously important.	• What exactly is impossible?
• Unfortunately, it's not going to matter regardless.	• To whom exactly is it obvious?
	• What exactly is important?
	• Unfortunately for whom?
	• What is unfortunate?

7. People sometimes limit themselves by regarding on-going processes, which they can influence and even control, as complete, uncontrollable and unchangeable facts of life. When you hear yourself thinking of situations as unchangeable or as carved in stone, then use these new responses:

Self-limiting comment: "There is no good reason for their refusal."

New response: "What is it exactly that they have been refusing to do?"

EXAMPLES OF SELF-LIMITING COMMENTS	NEW RESPONSES
• Their refusal to do anything about it is adding to my problem.	• They're refusing to do what exactly?
• My perceptions have been correct all along.	• What exactly have I been confusing?
• My financial situation is getting me down.	• I'm deciding what exactly?
• I'm not getting any cooperation.	• What is it that I'm really deciding?
	• Who exactly isn't cooperating?

EXAMPLES OF SELF-LIMITING COMMENTS (CONTINUED)	**NEW RESPONSES**
• My decision not to return to work is causing problems.	• What am I really anxious about?
• My anxiety keeps me stuck.	• What exactly about my financial situation is getting me down?
• My confusion makes me procrastinate.	

8. When you find yourself playing the game, "Ain't it awful" with respect to events in your life, then use these new responses:

Self-limiting comment: "This situation is much worse."

New response: "This situation is much worse than what?"

NOTE: Worse than what exactly? Is the situation worse . . .

• Than other situations I have faced?

• Than this situation used to be?

• Than someone else's situation?

EXAMPLES OF SELF-LIMITING COMMENTS	**NEW RESPONSES**
• This is much harder.	• Compared with what? More than what? Etc.
• This is the most difficult.	
• This is the best approach.	• Harder for me to manage than when?
• That's much more important to me.	• The hardest with respect to what?
• It's harder for me now to manage.	• More important to me than what?
	• A better approach than what?

9. When you find yourself using your opinions about other people and their actions or about circumstances as excuses not to act, then use these new responses:

Self-limiting comment: "No one can work with this creditor; he refused to postpone my payments until I find a job."

New response: "Because he wouldn't postpone my payments means that I can't work with him?"

EXAMPLES OF SELF-LIMITING COMMENTS	NEW RESPONSES
• They don't care; they never return my phone calls.	• Because they never return my phone calls means that they don't care? What else could it mean?
• He doesn't respect me; he never looks me in the eye when he's talking to me.	• Not looking me in the eye means that he doesn't respect me? What else could it mean?

SELF-TALK TO MOTIVATE YOURSELF AND TO REVEAL CHOICES

The following self-talk is particularly useful in challenging your habitual thinking and responses that have kept you from making progress. The example will motivate you and open additional choices and possibilities for you.

Miracle question. Ask yourself, "What will life be like if this problem were solved when I wake up tomorrow morning?" This is a very important question and a most difficult one to answer, because most likely you have never imagined what your life would be like without the problem.

Practice: After the bold type insert your own particular goal.
(The statements in parentheses are merely suggestions).

"How will my life be different when . . . (I have all of my bills paid off, have some savings and are no longer worried about my financial situation)?"

_____

_____

_____

"As I begin getting my life organized by setting up a filing system for my important papers this week I will . . . (pay particular attention to papers and records that I need to keep and those that I need to discard)."

_____

_____

_____

"When I am looking carefully for papers and records I need to keep when I set up my filing system I will . . . (see that I have made some useful and not so useful purchases, and as I do this, remember what I was thinking about at the time)."

_____

_____

_____

"Is there anything that could stop me from carrying out my wish to . . . (end my financial worries by creating a spending plan)?"

_____

_____

_____

"Do I think that paying off the entire balance on my credit card statement each month . . . (allows me to notice how much more money I have to use for other purposes and to save)?"

_____

_____

_____

"I'm wondering whether the second or third time I find myself . . . (preparing a list before grocery shopping will seem different from the first time)?"

_____

_____

_____

"How will my children respond . . . (when they see me and my wife/husband talking calmly about money as we pay our bills together)?"

_____

_____

_____

Counterexamples. Find just one exception to your most cherished "I can't . . ." belief, and it opens up a whole world of possibilities and positive outcomes. Finding some point in your life when you already have done it (or something similar) successfully can empower you to take action on your problem now.

Simultaneous conflicting tasks. Sometimes people have particular beliefs or engage in actions or tasks that conflict with each other and keep them from accomplishing either one. In such cases, it is important to recognize when beliefs may conflict with each other. Make any such actions or tasks sequential rather than simultaneous, in this manner:

- "When will be the best time to do this, and when will be the best time to do the other?"
- "Since this task is preventing me from doing this other one, which of these tasks is more important right now and which should be done first?"

A higher priority. Finding a higher priority or more important reason than the one that you are now basing a belief or behavior on can open new choices. For example:

- "What's important or valuable about tracking my spending?" (What makes me want to track my spending?)
- "What's important or valuable about not tracking my spending?" (What stops me from tracking my spending?)
- Higher priority: "So gaining peace of mind for myself and my family is more important to me than the small amount of time that tracking my spending will require?"

Changing your choices. Simply changing the kind of choice can accomplish major changes as follows:

- "I don't think the problem can be solved."
- "It's not whether or not I'm going to solve that problem, but only how (or when)."

Comparisons. Comparing yourself and your circumstances to other people is inappropriate and will damage your self-esteem, because the circumstances are not the same, despite how they may appear.

When you change the ways that you talk to yourself about your financial circumstances, you will automatically change the ways you have thought about them and the ways you have habitually responded to them. When you challenge any negative beliefs, doubts or self-limitations you may have had about money, you dislodge and remove any obstacles in your path to financial progress. When you challenge inappropriate generalizations about yourself, money and your financial life, and specify what choices are available and what steps are possible, you have empowered yourself in ways that will absolutely succeed. That's why these new ways of talking to yourself are so very important.

4.

ELIMINATING MONEY CONFLICTS

SELF-CONFLICTS ABOUT MONEY

People experiencing financial problems sometimes have mixed emotions or beliefs about money and what it means to be in control of it. Without identifying and resolving these self-conflicts, financial problems can persist indefinitely. If you unconsciously link money to fear or failure, believe that gaining better financial control means sacrificing your spirituality, that seeking financial security and prosperity equals greed or selfishness, or that anyone with money has taken advantage of others to get it, then these beliefs will sabotage your own financial progress and cause financial problems. This will happen despite the number of books you read or financial seminars you attend. The following kinds of self-talk show such self-conflicts:

- "I don't know what to do; part of me wants . . . , but another part of me wants . . ."

- "On the one hand I think (want) . . . , but on the other hand . . ."

- "I'm mixed up; sometimes I want . . . , but at other times . . ."

- "At the time I go shopping, it seems okay, but then later, I feel (think) . . ."

- "I just don't trust myself to . . . ."

- "I know I should get my financial life together, but . . . "

Just as we all have many different roles in life, there are many different parts to our personality as well. Certain parts of us control our beliefs and direct our actions in certain situations. There is a part of us that enjoys having a good time, a part that is serious when necessary, a part that is gentle and a part that is creative. There is also a part that may occasionally be insensitive or stubborn. There may be a part that acts in a way that is not helpful or even contrary to our own best interests in certain situations. At certain times or in certain situations, one of these parts may be responsible for a specific problem-causing behavior. Such a self-defeating response is hardly a complete description of what kind of person we are. All of us from time to time say, "Why did I do that? What made me do that? I know better than to do that!"

People often say they want to change, but deep down believe that maintaining the old beliefs, habits or choices gives them something they could not get any other way. A person may spend money to gain attention or to control others. To resolve this, they must find new ways to get their needs met. There must be something they want more, an overriding or higher priority than whatever they believe they are getting from continuing the problem-causing belief, habit or choice.

Each part of us, even the part that we label bad or harmful, has a positive intention or purpose that is, in some way, trying to take care of us. What people do afterwards though is to say, "I don't like that part of me. I don't like myself when I do that. I need to get rid of the part of me that is making me do this." We quickly forget that we didn't object when the unwanted behavior was happening. Then we didn't mind at all. It is only afterwards that we feel guilty and beat up on ourselves. We say such things as, "I need to stop that," or "I need to get rid of the part of me that is causing me to do that." Unfortunately, this kind of response does not help; it only causes self-conflict and lowers self-esteem. There are several steps you can take to change your self-defeating behavior.

First, express appreciation for the positive intention. Self-conflict will persist until you first recognize the positive intention or purpose of the part of you that is causing it. In your self-talk, express your appreciation to that part of you for taking care of you in that manner. This will resolve the self-conflict and verbal battle with yourself that is keeping you stuck in the unwanted problem-causing behavior.

Next, find other ways of satisfying the same intention. Find ways of stopping your pattern of indulging in self-defeating actions and then "beating yourself up" afterwards. Ask the part of you controlling the unwanted behavior if it would be willing to experiment with new ways of satisfying this same positive intention of taking care of you.

Then ask the creative part of yourself to identify new choices. Pause for several minutes, allowing your creative part to identify three new ways that will satisfy the same positive intention for you as the old unwanted habit did. Check these three choices out with the part that had been controlling the unwanted habit. Ask if it would be willing, in the weeks to come, to use one or more of these new choices to serve the same positive intentions as before. Finally, visualize yourself in the coming weeks using these new choices in different contexts or situations where the unwanted behavior previously happened. Fully experience how this looks, sounds and feels.

Use the following example to better understand how this method for change works. Let's assume that your spending is out of control, and that you get upset with yourself afterwards. As you engage in this positive and healing self-talk use a tape recorder, go slowly and give yourself time to develop mental images and feelings with each comment.

1. "First, I know that my spending problem is only one small part of me, that I have many other parts that are in control most of the time. I am a good spouse, a good parent, an excellent teacher, an effective businessperson [fill in other parts of yourself]."

2. "I know that the part of me that seems to control those spending sprees really has a positive intention. It wants to protect me or to take care of me somehow. The part of me that kicks me after each spending spree also has the best intentions at the time. It is really only trying to take care of me in ways that seem to give me pleasure at the time it is happening."

3. "At the time it is happening and I am off on one of those spending sprees, I haven't objected, have I? It's only afterwards that I beat up on myself for doing the only thing that part of me knows how to do to take care of me."

4. "Because I kick that part of me for trying to take care of me in that way, I have set up a conflict in myself. And since that conflict is going on inside me, I will continue that pattern of uncontrolled

spending and beating up on myself afterwards. It's time now that I end the conflict."

5. "First, I need to thank that part of me that has been causing that uncontrolled spending for trying to take care of me in that way."

6. "Next, I need to ask that part of me if it would be willing to experiment with three new ways of taking care of me at least as well as spending tried to do, if new ways can be found: 'Would you be willing to experiment with three new ways of taking care of yourself other than by spending money?'"

7. "Now, I want that very creative part of me to come up with several new ways of taking care of me that would be at least as effective as that old way of spending money uncontrollably. [Be quiet and listen within for suggestions.] Okay, that is one; there's another; and there's a third new way."

8. "Now, I would like to know if that part of me that has been causing me to spend money would be willing to experiment with these new ways of taking care of me at least as well as spending has. Would you do this for me in the days and weeks to come?"

9. "Now, I am actually seeing myself using each of these new ways and noticing how this looks, sounds and feels in different situations where I would have spent money before."

10. "How does this look, sound and feel? I thank all of my parts for cooperating in this joint project to take even better care of me than before. I thank all of my parts for cooperating with each other in doing this for me."

11. "Is there any other part of me that objects to what new things we're going to do? If not, okay. If so, what adjustment can we make to take care of that objection?"

This sequence of self-talk is highly effective in making peace with yourself and ending the self-defeating conflict that may be preventing your financial progress. Do it and experience for yourself how effective you can be!

SPENDING OUT OF CONTROL

As many as one out of five people has some problems controlling their spending and for half of these (10%), it is out of control. In *Money* magazine's 1987 poll of people's financial habits, two out of three people said they go on shopping sprees, and one in five goes shopping when depressed. These figures should surprise no one in view of the hidden nature of compulsive spending. Confronting compulsive spenders with their behavior leads them to heavy denial. Self-assessment 6 in Chapter 10 will enable you to assess the amount of control you have of your spending.

The extent of compulsive spending is only now becoming known and understood because first, there has been no clear definition of it. Second, it has been difficult to identify. And third, compulsive spenders are either unaware of it or strongly deny it. What are the differences among spontaneous, impulsive and compulsive spending? The definition of spontaneous, in a leading dictionary, is "acting or activated without deliberation." Spontaneous and impulsive are synonymous. Compulsion is defined as "an irresistible impulse to perform an irrational act," and compulsive is synonymous with obsessive.

To occasionally spend money spontaneously or impulsively is human nature, and to sometimes buy something to cheer oneself up is healthy. Even occasional excess is harmless. The question is, at what point does spending get out of control. Spending is compulsive or out of control when it has become someone's customary way of achieving self-esteem or of dealing with stress or emotional distress. Compulsive spenders often hide their purchases from their families, just as an alcoholic will hide a bottle or an addict will hide drugs. Often, purchases do not have the store tags removed and will never be used.

Spending also is compulsive if it is done to escape reality, to create a fantasy life with the objects purchased or with the shopping process itself. So-called spontaneous spending becomes harmful when financial and other subsequent problems outweigh any momentary positive feelings at the time of spending. It is compulsive if it results in financial problems, chronic worry and/or guilt, or if it interferes with responsibilities or relationships with others. Spending is compulsive when you admit or suggest that you no longer have control of it. *Simply stated, spending is out of control when you begin to abuse yourself or your loved ones with it.*

Our society still considers uncontrolled spending acceptable and laughs it off with clichés such as "retail therapy" or "When the going gets tough, the tough go shopping." Our society encourages excessive spending with such excuses as "you can have it all," "you owe it to yourself," "always get the best" and "everybody does it."

If you regard yourself as a free spirit and claim to spend money spontaneously or freely without worrying or without any spending plan, you probably worry about money. It probably interferes with your work, relationships, play, sleep and even your health. It may worry your loved ones even more than it worries you, as they watch what it is doing to you and to those who care about you.

Although compulsive spending does not lead to a physical addiction as does alcohol or drugs, it can be difficult to identify and treat because of the prevailing attitudes mentioned above. Therefore, it may not be taken seriously. Like they do with other forms of addiction, people strongly deny it and recognize that they have a problem only after it has destroyed marriages and other relationships. It has resulted in repossession, wage garnishment, lawsuits and even job loss. Like other addicts, compulsive spenders often are prone to dual addictions such as overeating or substance abuse along with their spending problem. Many women who are compulsive spenders are also noticeably overweight or bulimic. During the compulsive spender's childhood, the parents were likely to have

- been compulsive role models from whom the child learned that spending was an acceptable way of coping with negative emotions or the stresses of life;

- been extreme in using money, either very impulsive and careless with it or very stingy with it;

- been addicted in one or more ways, such as to alcohol, drugs, overeating or compulsive gambling;

- had exceptionally high expectations of their children or made them feel inferior or inadequate; or

- had rigid religious beliefs in which shopping, spending and eating were the only acceptable ways of self-gratification and self-nurturing.

When they were children, some compulsive spenders felt that there was never enough food or other necessities to go around. As adults, they are unable to delay gratification and feel that they must buy what they want now, otherwise they'll never get it later. They suffered emotional deprivation during childhood. They continue to try to compensate by getting things that make them feel good, accepted or powerful. As a result of their childhood experience compulsive spenders are likely to have feelings of low self-esteem, powerlessness, insecurity or abandonment.

Compulsive spenders spend money to compensate for things they feel are missing in their lives or to react to interpersonal problems at home or at work. They may feel thwarted or shackled, which results in unbridled spending. Thus, as with other forms of compulsive behavior, identity issues usually underlie the behavior. Typical identity issues are the inability to take control of their lives, the inability to stand up for themselves and the desire to be strong, independent, respected, accepted, appreciated, attractive, loved, safe, secure or protected.

REGAINING CONTROL OF SPENDING

People who are trying to gain better financial control may feel that more willpower, self-discipline or hard work is the answer. If this does not work, they feel a sense of conflict and failure. However, willpower depends on the conscious mind, while compulsive spending is reactive behavior outside of conscious awareness. If people are programmed from childhood to believe that they cannot deal with stress or emotional upsets except through shopping, and if they believe that compulsive spending is okay, then willpower, discipline and hard work are not going to help. Dysfunctional money attitudes and habits become progressively worse. Fortunately, gaining control of your spending through incremental changes is also progressive. Gaining control encourages you and makes it easier to take further steps. It has a positive rippling effect throughout your financial life.

To start gaining control of the compulsive spending pattern, you need to first identify and understand what triggers it. You need to know how you react to these triggers. A danger signal that warns of compulsive spending is a feeling of extreme urgency to find and buy a particular item, a feeling that you must have something immediately. Notice the physical tension in your body when you get such a feeling of urgency. Whatever way you choose to deal with the problem, you must reduce the physical tension that alerts you to an impending spending binge. Put your hand on the tense area of your body and then by moving your hand, move this physical tension to another area of your body. Preferably move it to where you feel creativity and choices. This simple technique can interrupt the physical tension that accompanies the compulsive spending.

Another way to reduce this physical tension is through deep breathing, visualization and positive verbal affirmations. These can be done at the first sign of the compulsion to go shopping. Another easy and effective way to do this is to dissociate with the stress-producing triggering event. In disassociating, imagine seeing the stress-producing or triggering event as though it was occurring on a movie or television screen. Thus, by stepping out of the picture and gaining a different (dissociated) perspective, you are interrupting the emotion and tension-spending sequence. This works best when combined with deep breathing, relaxation and even meditation. Dissociating by playing mental movies of these events backward and forward, then changing the timing and sequencing of the images of the stress-producing events, is effective in reducing the physical tension that signals the onset of the compulsive spending.

Spending money compulsively is an attempt to fill emptiness from the outside, but inner emptiness can only be filled from the inside. Ask yourself, "What need am I trying to fill here? Is there another way that I can do this without spending money?" You can sometimes find out why you compulsively spend simply by asking yourself, "What does this do for me? What do I get from it that is still important to me?" Once you have identified what this reward is and what it does for you, then you can find other ways that will satisfy this need without causing the spending problem. These are rewards that compulsive spenders report from spending:

- Self-esteem
- A sense of importance, respect or power
- Attention

- Acceptance, being part of an "in" group
- Feeling free and independent
- Fantasy

Sometimes people are not consciously aware of what rewards they get from compulsive spending or what might be causing it. Although they may not be consciously aware of it, subconsciously they are. In the conflict between a person's conscious and subconscious awareness over compulsive spending, the subconscious always wins and the person compulsively spends. If people are not consciously aware of what they are getting from the problem-causing behavior, the following approach can be helpful:

Ask yourself what feeling you're getting from the experience. What is the feeling that you are experiencing as you find yourself spending? What does this do for you? Your answer will have nothing to do with the need for the item or service about to be purchased. You will most likely experience one or more of the feelings listed above. Some compulsive spenders even report feelings of excitement, a "high," and even a momentary dizziness or tingling sensation. Once you identify this, then other, more suitable and less costly ways can be found to satisfy these needs and get these feelings without any of the subsequent consequences and self-blame.

OTHER STEPS TO GET SPENDING UNDER CONTROL

Keep a diary or log of your successes with these suggestions. Follow this plan for a month. Notice what you're experiencing and feeling and record it in your diary or log.

1. Begin by limiting your shopping to the odd-numbered days of the week (first, third and fifth day) for the first week. In the second week, limit your shopping to the even-numbered days of the week (second, fourth and sixth day). In the third week, limit your shopping to the first, third and fifth day of the week again. On the fourth week, limit it to the second, fourth and sixth day of the

week as before. Pay close attention to what you're experiencing and feeling, and jot these things down in a notebook. At the end of the month, review what you have jotted down.

2. Track your daily spending, save all your receipts and record every penny spent at the end of each day.

3. Always shop with a prepared list.

4. Take only enough money for items on your list; leave your credit cards at home.

5. If a sudden impulse to shop occurs, stop what you're doing immediately. Close your eyes for a few moments and breathe deeply. If you can find a few minutes to meditate, this is even better. Focus all of your attention on your breathing. If you feel physical tension anywhere in your body, place the palm of your hand on it and as you breathe deeply, move your hand and with it the tension to some other part of your body. Continue to breathe deeply or to meditate until you can no longer feel the tension. As you do this, visualize yourself doing something else, such as participating in some other activity that you enjoy.

Select and use any three of the following suggestions for a month. Notice what you're experiencing and feeling, and record this in your diary or log.

1. Destroy your credit cards or put them in an ice cube tray, cover them with water and freeze them.

2. Avoid shopping alone or with persons who encourage you to buy things when shopping with them.

3. When facing a buying decision involving two or more choices, discipline yourself to buy only one, despite how much you may like them all.

4. If you purchase something you do not like or that is unsuitable, take it back immediately.

5. Always show your family your purchases. Avoid hiding any item you buy except gifts to others.

6. Establish a plan of activity for the weekend that includes setting your alarm and getting up no later than one hour past your normal wake-up time.

7. Join a support group, but only if the group makes you feel confident about controlling or eliminating your problem. If not, quit immediately.

8. Begin a bill reduction program and set a goal of paying off all of your bills or debts by a certain date.

9. Have a garage sale to launch your recovery program and clear closets of things you no longer want or use. Sell such items in classified ads, using the money to pay bills and debts.

10. Take a course in assertiveness. There are better ways of feeling assertive and in control than by spending money. Compulsive spenders need to find other ways of dealing with stress, anger, frustration, and other negative events and feelings than by shopping and spending money.

FINDING ALTERNATIVES

Finally, no behavioral change can be based on self-denial or deprivation. Depriving oneself of something without fully understanding what that something does (what feeling one gets from it) is doomed to failure from the start. Instead, find an equally acceptable alternative that will fulfill or satisfy that needed something.

Just as an alcoholic's first spending priority is alcohol and a drug addict's is the next fix, a compulsive spender focuses on the next shopping spree. Compulsive spenders need a new focus to replace their reliance upon compulsive spending. In Figure 4.1 are 77 specific ideas for self-nurturing, developed in a stress management support group at Southern Illinois University. Most people can find several activities on this list that are better alternatives than shopping and spending. Choose three from the list in Figure 4.1.

Figure 4.1   Ideas for Self-Nurturing

- Listen to my favorite music.
- Enjoy a long, warm bubble bath.
- Go for a walk.
- Share a hug with a loved one.
- Relax outside.
- Exercise (of my choice).
- Pray.
- Attend a caring support group.
- Practice diaphragmatic breathing.
- Do stretching exercises.
- Reflect on my positive qualities: "I am . . . "
- Watch the sunrise/sunset.
- Laugh.
- Concentrate on a relaxing scene.
- Create a collage representing "the real me."
- Receive a message.
- Reflect on "I appreciate . . . "
- Write my thoughts and feelings in a personal journal.
- Attend a favorite athletic event.
- Do something adventurous (e.g., skydiving).
- Read a special book or magazine.
- Sing/hum/whistle a happy tune.
- Swing/slide/teeter totter.
- Play a musical instrument.
- Meditate.
- Work with plants (gardening).
- Learn a new skill.
- Work out with weights or equipment.
- Ride a bike or motorcycle.
- Make myself a nutritious meal.
- Draw/paint a picture.
- Swim/float/wade/relax in a pool/ on the beach.
- Do aerobics/dance.
- See a special play, movie or concert.
- Visit a special place I enjoy.
- Smile/Say: "I Love You."
- Take time to smell the roses (and other flowers I enjoy)!
- Imagine myself achieving my goals and dreams.
- Go horseback riding.
- Reflect on "my most enjoyable memories."
- Enjoy a relaxing nap.
- Visit a museum/art gallery.
- Practice yoga.
- Relax in a whirlpool/sauna.
- Enjoy a cool, refreshing glass of water or fruit juice.
- Enjoy the beauty of nature.
- Count my blessings: "I am thankful for . . . "
- Play as I did as a child.
- Star gaze.
- Volunteer in your community.
- Daydream.
- Tell myself the loving words I want to hear from others.
- Attend a special workshop.
- Go sailing/paddle boating.
- Reward myself with a special gift I can afford.
- Take myself on a vacation.
- Create with clay/pottery.
- Practice positive affirmations.
- Pet an animal.
- Watch my favorite TV show.
- Reflect on my successes: "I can . . . "
- Write a poem expressing my feelings.
- Make a bouquet of flowers.

Figure 4.1   Ideas for Self-Nurturing   (Continued)

- RELAX: watch the clouds.
- Make myself something nice.
- Visit a park/woods/forest.
- Read positive, motivational literature.
- Reflect on "What I value most in life!"
- Phone a special friend.
- Picnic in a beautiful setting
- Enjoy a gourmet cup of herbal tea/decaf coffee.

- Participate in a favorite sport/game/recreation.
- Practice a relaxation exercise (or listen to relaxation tapes).
- Practice the art of forgiveness.
- Treat myself to a nutritious meal at a favorite restaurant.
- Participate in a hobby.
- Create my own unique list of self-nurturing activities

Source: Reprinted from Guidepost, vol. 33, no. 9, pp. 11. ©ACA. Reprinted with permission. No further reproduction authorized without written permission of the American Counseling Association.

CONFLICTS OF A COUPLE

This section is intended for use by couples. If this doesn't apply to you, simply skip ahead to Chapter 5. If you are having money conflicts in your marriage, it will be more helpful for you and your spouse to think of them in terms of reactions in your interactions with each other. Do not think of them in terms of who is at fault or is causing problems. Usually, it's your reactions to each other's attitudes and actions that are creating or worsening financial conflicts.

For some people, money represents power and being right about money represents having or gaining power. They make many of their financial decisions to prove this power or to gain or maintain control of others, particularly in relationships. Money conflicts usually revolve around power struggles. They result in spouses retaliating either with the use of money, sex or in another way to prove their power.

Conflict also can come from fear, particularly when people fear not having enough money for something that they believe they need or value highly. People often defend most vigorously those beliefs and values about money that they are not really sure about. When they are clear about their beliefs, they rarely feel the need to defend them.

A relationship can change as a person changes his or her interactions with the other about money. A couple is an interacting system.

No matter how small a change it is, when one person changes anything in the relationship, the other spouse will adapt in some way to the change made. Upon seeing the growing skill of a spouse's handling of finances, the other spouse often begins doing things differently. For couples, a key task can have a rippling effect in the way that they talk with each other about money. Small steps will help you change the way you think about and use money and become building blocks for major changes. Small steps change stumbling blocks into building blocks!

Here are three key tasks that you and your spouse can do to reduce any conflicts about money and improve your communication. Pay close attention to what you notice as you carry out these tasks:

1. Paying Bills Together

Simply changing when and how you and your spouse pay your monthly bills can jump start changes in how you talk about money. This can lead to further changes. Changing the timing and procedure with which you pay bills enables both of you to see how much certain expenses actually are, and where your money is going. It will help you talk more calmly about specific amounts rather than about vague uncertainties. It helps in identifying ways to reduce expenses, plan spending and develop better control of your money so it can be used for what is really important to you.

1. Both of you agree that on a certain day this month you will sit together to pay your monthly bills. This should preferably be at a time when you are not hurried or will not be interrupted.

2. One spouse writes out the checks for the bills and hands the bills and checks to the other spouse who then writes the account numbers on the checks, puts them in the envelope with the bills, writes the addresses, seals and stamps the envelopes.

3. The next month, reverse these roles.

2. Comparing Beliefs and Values about Money

1. Jot down your individual answers to the following questions:
   "How would I know that my spouse has the same values about money as I do? What attitudes, habits and actions would show me that she or he has the same beliefs?" (List these and be as specific as possible.)

2. Then, compare your individual lists. If you're having conflicts about money, there will be little if any overlap. If one list is long while the other has little or nothing listed, it may mean that the one with little or nothing may be using money issues to hide other issues in the relationship.

3. You then need to discuss with each other the similarities and differences in your two lists, beginning with the similarities.

3. Catching Your Spouse Doing Something Right about Money

1. First, list things that you admire about your spouse's attitudes and habits regarding money. Then, list things that you dislike about your spouse's attitudes and habits about money.

2. Exchange lists with your spouse, beginning with what each of you likes about the other's money management attitudes and habits, then the things that you dislike about each other's money management attitudes and habits.

3. During the week, "catch your spouse doing something right" (something you like) with respect to money and jot it down in a notebook or on a pad of paper. See which one can record the most admirable things during the week. Depending on your financial situation, you can even set up some kind of reward. The reward might be that whoever catches the other doing the most admirable thing is taken out to dinner or gives over a household task to the other.

This will help you begin focusing on each other's admirable attitudes and habits with money instead of each other's mistakes. It can help you both to look for ways to do those things with money that the other likes. Soon, you will have established more positive attitudes and habits about money, and you will find fewer conflicts about it.

Remember, you cannot change other people and this includes your spouse. By focusing on what you can do and by controlling your own actions and responses, tiny changes will begin to occur. These small changes produce more changes in your financial situation, in your outlook about your financial situation and in your spouse's attitudes and actions as he or she adapts to the changes that you've made. By acting as if you have already resolved any money differences, you can often create these resolutions, even if your spouse does not cooperate at first. Ask yourself these three questions:

1. "What will I do if my spouse does not change?"

_____

_____

_____

2. "What is my spouse likely to see or hear me doing differently that will let him or her know that I'm becoming more competent and confident?"

_____

_____

_____

3. "What is my spouse likely to see or hear me doing differently that will let him or her know that I'm not only doing my share, but can do it without him or her?"

_____

_____

_____

As you begin dealing with money in these new ways, focus on and jot down what may be working that you want to continue. Do not focus on trying to get your spouse to change.

Money tips for couples. Twelve steps for money harmony:

1. If both husband and wife work, most couples find it easier to have a joint household account for routine expenses and a separate personal account for each. Discuss whether you both will contribute equally to the joint account or if you will each contribute in proportion to your respective incomes.

2. Set aside a regular time for discussion of money matters, preferably a day when neither of you has to work. By scheduling regular times for doing this, less time will be necessary and problems avoided. You will find such discussions shorter, calmer and more productive if you discuss figures on paper.

3. Avoid blaming each other for financial problems. Rigid attitudes, beliefs or expectations about how you think your spouse should act will stifle your financial happiness and progress. It will cause problems in other areas of your lives as well.

4. Avoid mentioning how your parents or friends handle money. It is irrelevant and will make it more difficult for you both to reach mutually acceptable financial decisions.

5. Avoid surprises; they are often misinterpreted and cause problems. Let each other know what is going on financially.

6. Make sure that each of you has a credit card in your own name, whether it was obtained before or after your marriage. Two good individual credit histories are better than one joint history when you apply for a loan. If one of you has a blemished credit record, the other's clean record can be a great advantage.

7. From time to time, look at other ways of managing your money better. It is especially important if there is a change in job status that has or might lead to a change in income and expenses.

8. Divide responsibilities for regular financial tasks as evenly as possible, so that neither of you feels you're shouldering all of the burden. Refusing to take an interest in financial matters can be just as destructive to your financial communication as insisting on complete control in such matters.

9. Make sure that you both discuss and agree about the use of any expected or unexpected windfall. If one spouse receives a windfall of money and unilaterally makes a decision about its use, it can damage the trust you have established and harm your entire relationship.

10. Involve your children in your family financial discussions and decisions as much as possible. Children usually want to be involved in family financial decisions that affect them, such as plans for a vacation or whether to buy a new television or a VCR. They also prefer to know about any financial problems that you may be facing. It is a myth to think that you are sheltering your children from such problems. They find out about them anyway and are even more frightened and insecure when they see you attempting to hide such problems from them.

11. If you or your spouse's spending has gotten out of control or if one of you has constant or frequent worries about money that you cannot resolve together, seek help from a professional financial counselor.

12. Develop some short- and long-range financial goals together.

Figure 4.2　Financial Values and Beliefs for Couples

This self-assessment will help you and the person with whom you live see how similar you are in your values and beliefs about money, and how well you both communicate about it. It also will help you clarify your own values and beliefs about money.

Instructions:

Partner A:　Circle the number to the *left* of each statement with which you agree or which may apply to you and your situation.

Partner B:　Circle the number to the *right* of each statement with which you agree or which may apply to you and your situation.

Partner A	I. Couple Financial Communication Scale	Partner B
1.	A serious discussion about money is a good way to damage a loving relationship.	1.
2.	My partner and I disagree on how much money should be spent for what.	2.
3.	My partner and I make important financial decisions about money which affect us both without first consulting each other.	3.
4.	My partner and I are unable to reach satisfactory compromises in differences of opinions about the use of money.	4.
5.	I usually am the one who agrees or gives in when we make financial decisions despite uneasiness or misgivings about the decision.	5.
6.	My partner gives me the silent treatment when we are having a financial problem.	6.
7.	My partner jokes or makes comments about my use or management of money that make me feel bad.	7.
8.	If I have a troublesome financial problem, I prefer to work it out myself rather than burden my partner about it.	8.
9.	My partner and I argue about money.	9.
10.	My partner has no confidence in my ability to handle our money.	10.

Figure 4.2   Financial Values and Beliefs for Couples (Continued)

Partner A	II. Financial Satisfaction Scale	Partner B
1.	I am satisfied with our financial position or situation.	1.
2.	I am satisfied with how we handle financial role responsibilities in our relationship.	2.
3.	I am satisfied about how we make financial decisions and resolve financial conflicts.	3.
4.	My partner is not a spendthrift or stingy.	4.
5.	Two incomes are not necessary for us to make it financially.	5.
6.	My prior expectations about my financial lifestyle have turned out to be fairly accurate.	6.
7.	I feel adequate when it comes to managing money.	7.
8.	I can handle financial problems as well as my partner.	8.
9.	I don't worry about money.	9.
10.	I don't feel trapped by a lack of money.	10.

Partner A	III. Roles	Partner B
1.	Even if both partners are working, men should pay the bills.	1.
2.	Even if both partners are working, men should pick up the check when they go out.	2.
3.	If a man pays the bills and picks up the checks, then he should make the decisions about the money.	3.
4.	Women and men should share responsibilities and learn from each other.	4.
5.	Most women are raised to be wives and mothers, not to be self-supporting.	5.
6.	Men should be providers and women should be caretakers and nurturers.	6.
7.	Men have the responsibility of protecting their wives from day to day concerns about money.	7.
8.	Men and women owe it to themselves and to their future children not to become parents unless they are able to earn a living.	8.
9.	Financially independent women are unattractive to men and may even scare men.	9.
10.	It's better for people to get married only after they have lived independently.	10.

Figure 4.2 Financial Values and Beliefs for Couples (Continued)

Partner A	IV. Attitudes	Partner B
1.	I have set clear and specific financial goals to guide me.	1.
2.	Budgets limit my flexibility in handling money.	2.
3.	Money can solve most of my problems.	3.
4.	I feel inadequate compared to others who have more money than I do.	4.
5.	I feel more important than those who have less money than I do.	5.
6.	I feel the need to buy things to impress other people.	6.
7.	I have difficulty making decisions about spending money.	7.
8.	Paying off loans and using as little credit as necessary makes good financial sense.	8.
9.	Partners should pool their money rather than keep separate bank accounts.	9.
10.	Children are well worth the expense.	10.

Partner A	V. Spending Habits	Partner B
1.	I spend money to compensate for other things that are lacking in my life.	1.
2.	I spend more than usual when I am upset, worried, depressed or bored.	2.
3.	I often have regrets after I have purchased something.	3.
4.	My buying is usually spontaneous rather than planned.	4.
5.	I often spend money impulsively.	5.
6.	If I have money left over at the end of the month, I spend rather than save it.	6.
7.	I buy the most expensive item available that I can afford at the time.	7.
8.	I usually buy well-known name brands instead of private brands.	8.
9.	I usually don't take advantage of sales or specials.	9.
10.	I sometimes buy things I don't need or want because they are on sale.	10.

Figure 4.2   Financial Values and Beliefs for Couples (Continued)

Interpreting Your Responses

1. After you and your partner have circled the numbers of your responses on the left and right of each statement, identify those statements on which you agreed and those on which you disagreed. Total the number of those statements on which you agreed and total those on which you disagreed and write them in the boxes below.

2. In which of the five areas do you and your partner most agree. Enter the "agree" totals for each of the five sections in Column A.

3. In which of the five areas do you and your partner disagree. Enter the "disagree" totals for each of the five sections in Column B.

4. On which specific statements (values and beliefs) do you agree. Enter the numbers of specific statements in Column C.

5. On which specific statements (values and beliefs) do you disagree. Enter the numbers of specific statements in Column D.

	A. Tend to Agree (Statement Totals)	B. Tend to Disagree (Statement Totals)	C. Specific Values/ Beliefs on Which We Agree (List Statement Number)	D. Specific Values/ Beliefs on Which We Disagree (List Statement Number)
I. Communication				
II. Satisfaction				
III. Roles				
IV. Attitudes				
V. Habits				

5.

STEPPING STONES TO FINANCIAL SUCCESS

When Bill and Gloria Thompson first came to see me, I could tell they were very stressed. Despite the fact that they both worked and had good incomes—he worked for the city and she was a school teacher—they were living a hand-to-mouth lifestyle. They called themselves free spirits, claiming, "When we have it, we spend it; when we don't have it, we don't spend it. It's as simple as that." However, they found themselves more and more anxious, worried and fighting over money issues.

The Thompsons had large credit card balances. Like so many people, they said that credit cards gave them freedom to do what they wished, when they wished. At the same time, they complained that they didn't seem to be able to do some other things that were important to them, such as save money for their two children's educations and put a few dollars away for retirement. Their spending pattern could best be characterized as "crisis spending." Because they didn't plan how best to use their income, they often found themselves dealing with financial emergencies. Any unexpected expense, no matter how small, upset them. They labeled a recent car repair, followed by an unexpected medical expense as bad breaks, saying that things were going just fine until bad luck dealt them these back-to-back blows.

The Thompsons were making minimum payments of over $225 a month on their credit cards. We discovered that Bill needed to work two days a month and Gloria one day just to pay the interest on their credit card bills without even reducing the amount they owed. When I showed them this and said, "How would you both like to come to work for me for a couple of days each month without being paid?" They quickly got the point.

Meanwhile, they were not participating in their employers' 401(k) tax-deferred retirement plans. They were missing an excellent opportunity to lower their taxes, set aside money for retirement and earn extra income through a 10 percent matching contribution plan. Their excuse was simply that they couldn't afford to participate under their present financial situation. "Perhaps later," they said, "when things get better."

Like many people, they mistakenly believed that by claiming no deductions on their federal and state income taxes, they could receive a $2,400 tax refund and be ahead of the game. With this money they caught up on overdue bills, bought needed things for the house, themselves and their children, and paid for part of a vacation while borrowing money for the rest of it. I asked them, "What would you say to someone who suggested that you give him over $200 a month to hold for you until the following year, interest-free?" They laughed and said, "We'd say that person must be crazy or kidding."

They told me they didn't want any more worry, stress or arguments over money, yet they were averse to changing their lifestyle. "If you continue to do what you've been doing," I said, "you'll continue to get what you've been getting—more of the same." They were stunned. I added, "To gain financial freedom you don't have to change who you are or deprive yourself of what you want. You simply need to find out what you really want most and begin doing some things differently. While this may seem like a difficult task, you may find that the solution is easier than continuing to have the problem."

The Thompsons held a view shared by many people who claim they can't seem to get ahead. Each time they would think of some step to take, they would immediately discard it as being just a drop in the bucket and not enough to really matter. Yet financial progress is made in very small steps taken consistently over a period of time. Each so-called drop in the bucket is tremendously important, not only because it provides a few additional dollars but also because it empowers people and helps them establish positive momentum.

To help them deal with their immediate problems, the Thompsons and I created a plan to eliminate some of their financial worries. Confronted with the reality of what they had been doing and the costliness of this unrestrained use of their credit cards, they devised the following plan to repay their credit cards and loans, and to gain control of their financial lives:

Increase tax exemptions. Since they had been getting tax refunds each year of over $2,400, this meant that they had withheld $200 too much in federal and state income taxes each month. They went to their payroll offices and changed the number of exemptions they took on their withholding (W-4). Since they were in the 28 percent tax bracket, each additional exemption provided them with an additional $59 in take-home pay. So, Mr. Thompson added two more withholding exemptions, and Mrs. Thompson added one more withholding exemption. Between them, they had $174 a month more to take home.

"Freeze" credit cards. They took their credit cards, put them in an ice cube tray, covered them with water and froze them with a vow that each card would remain in "deep freeze" until they had paid off the balance on that card. Then they listed their credit cards in order from the one with the highest interest rate to the one with the lowest interest rate. (*Note:* They could have also listed them in order from the lowest balance that they could pay the fastest, to the one that would take longer to pay off.) Then, with the additional $174 pay they now received each month, they used the "Power Pay" principle. Each month, as they paid off the first credit card, they would add that card's monthly payment to their usual payment on the next card and so on until all of the credit cards had been paid off. They continued doing this with their other debts, until all but their car loan and mortgage had been paid.

Assess health insurance needs. They both had their employers deduct their health insurance for the entire family. To be more economical, they looked at which health insurance plan provided the best benefits at the least cost. Then Mr. Thompson kept the insurance on himself, but dropped it on the rest of the family. This strategy saved them $60 a month.

Explore other health insurance options. Mr. and Mrs. Thompson found that their average spending totaled about $900 every year in out-of-pocket, unreimbursed medical expenses for themselves and their two children. However, Mrs. Thompson's employer provided a medical flex plan. Under this plan, employees can deduct an amount from each paycheck to be held in a special account for out-of-pocket medical expenses not reimbursed by their health insurance company. The deduction is in pre-tax dollars so it lowers their income tax obligation. Mrs. Thompson decided to deduct $75 tax-free each month from her paycheck and placed it into this medical flex spending account. No longer would out-of-pocket medical expenses create financial problems.

Reassess auto insurance. When I met them, Mr. and Mrs. Thompson had received a premium notice for their auto insurance policies indicating that their premiums on each car would be increased when the policies came up for renewal. Although Mr. Thompson had purchased this insurance from a relative, just out of curiosity he called three other auto insurance companies. All three quoted him a lower price for the same amount of insurance. One of the three was quite a bit lower, so Mr. Thompson changed his auto insurance company, doubled both the bodily and property liability coverage and raised the collision and comprehensive deductibles on both cars to the equivalent of one week's take-home pay. These changes actually improved their auto insurance coverage and saved them $240 a year ($20 a month).

What about the homeowner's policy? Mr. Thompson also switched his homeowner's insurance policy to his new auto insurance company, and received a discount on his homeowner's policy for doing so.

Take a look at life insurance needs. This in turn led Mr. Thompson to take a fresh look at his life insurance. He had been sold an expensive $100,000 cash value life insurance policy years before. With two small children, he needed much more insurance than this but claimed that he couldn't afford it. He had no disability insurance at all, despite the far greater risk of becoming disabled and the potentially devastating consequences that would have on his family. As he looked into this matter, he found that at his age he could buy term life insurance for about one-fifth the price of his cash value life insurance or five times the amount of life insurance that he had been paying for the cash value policy. After talking with Mrs. Thompson, they decided that he could double the amount of his life insurance and take out a disability policy, which would provide an income for his family if he became disabled, for less than what he had been paying on just the cash value policy.

Participate in employer 401(k) plans. Also, both Mr. and Mrs. Thompson signed up for their employers' 401(k) retirement plans. Since money placed into this plan is tax deductible, and since they were in the 28 percent tax bracket, their deductions for this retirement plan reduced their income taxes by 28 percent. Although they couldn't afford to put very much into this plan initially, as soon as their credit cards were paid off they began making the maximum payment allowable for these plans.

Pay off existing debts. As soon as they had paid off their credit cards and were contributing the maximum allowed to their 401(k) plans, they paid off their car loan. This freed-up $190 per month that could now be used for their next step.

Make extra mortgage payments. Mr. and Mrs. Thompson were able to complete all of the above steps in about 18 months from the time they started. They then began making extra payments on their mortgage each month and used additional cash from different sources to pay toward their mortgage as well. They didn't want to pay it off too quickly because their mortgage was an important tax deduction for them every year. Instead, they planned their payments in such a way that their mortgage would be paid off by the time they retired. If necessary, when their children enter college, they could arrange for a home equity loan to help pay for their children's college expenses.

While these steps helped to take care of their most pressing situations, the Thompsons needed to also work on an overall plan for changing the way they handled their finances. To help them achieve this new behavior toward their money, I gave them a copy of the plan in Chapter 10. A month later, I could tell by the way they walked into my office that something very positive had happened. Smiling broadly, Bill said, "Boy, what a difference in our lives. A month ago I would have said this wasn't even possible. We were surprised to find that we spend far less time now thinking about financial stuff than we did before." He added, "We decided to make the whole process a game, to make it fun instead of a chore."

FEELINGS THAT ACCOMPANY
FINANCIAL PROBLEMS

Feelings of loss of control or helplessness are common feelings that accompany financial problems. People who do not feel in control of their financial situations are often reactive, reacting to, rather than controlling events in their lives. One aspect of reactivity is to look to other people to make things better. People often change only when their financial problems become severe or some specific crisis has occurred. They look for something or someone to bail them out or rescue them.

Just earning more money will not end financial fears and worry, nor give you more freedom. You will enjoy more financial freedom and peace of mind as you develop more control of how you use money. Although you do not have to become a financial expert, you do need to get your financial life on track and pointed in a positive direction. People who do not control their financial lives most often find that this causes them to lose control of other parts of their lives also. Surprisingly, once people have gotten control of their finances, they find that they spend less time thinking about money.

Focusing on possible solutions is the key to resolving a financial problem and to improving your financial situation. Do not get bogged down in trying to explain what caused a problem or lack of progress. Trying to explain or justify how a financial problem occurred is *not* going to help solve it and wastes valuable time. It also causes you to mentally rehearse how to continue to have the problem. A vivid example of this was a recent news story about one of the best hitters in professional baseball. He was having a hitting slump and the slump was getting worse. One day his coach saw him sitting in a room watching videotapes of himself in the slump and getting more depressed. Fortunately, his coach spotted the trouble immediately. The coach told him to stop rehearsing his slump, and instead to start watching tapes of himself when he was in his full stride and hitting well. Once this hitter did so, his slump stopped almost immediately.

People unintentionally do this with money problems and financial situations as well. By focusing all of their attention on trying to discover what they did wrong, they simply become more adept at doing it the same way. People get stuck in their problems this way and end up feeling inadequate or like failures in dealing with money. You will find it much easier and faster to resolve a financial problem and improve your financial situation if you keep these five simple rules in mind:

1. If something you're doing is working, don't fix it, do more of it.

2. If something you're doing works a little, build on it.

3. If something you're doing isn't working, do something different, even if it seems strange or illogical.

4. Keep it simple.

5. No matter what you do, you can't fail. You'll just find that you didn't get the results you wanted and need to find another way.

Let's look at each of these important rules in more depth.

1. If something you're doing is working, don't change it, do more of it. How you handle your money, how you make daily decisions about paying your bills, how you spend it and how you divide it up for various purposes are important. Despite how badly you think your financial situation is, no matter how many mistakes you make with your money, there is something, probably several things that you are doing well. Focus on what you are doing with money that is okay and that is *not* causing problems.

If you keep focusing on what you want and take small steps to get it, then obstacles will start disappearing. On the other hand, if any obstacle seems too difficult, then it is probably telling you that there is a better way to accomplish your goal. Circumstances that you sometimes see as barriers will lead you in another direction that will turn out to be a better way to go. Obstacles are sometimes there to protect you, to keep you from taking action prematurely or to get you to pay attention to something you may have been missing.

2. If something you're doing works a little, build on it! Those areas of your life where there are no problems are areas where you're making effective decisions and handling money well. How can you build on or expand these successful areas? What are your beliefs, attitudes and habits in these successful aspects of your financial life? How do you talk to yourself when you're making these decisions and plans? What picture of yourself are you seeing? How can you extend these same beliefs, habits and self-confidence to handle any financial problems? Take a moment now to answer these questions in your mind. Get a mental picture as you answer, noticing how you talk to yourself during these times and how you feel.

3. If something you're doing isn't working, do something different, even if it seems awkward, strange or illogical! How many times have you heard the self-defeating cliché, "If at first you don't succeed, try, try again"? If doing something like always relying on credit, or enjoying yourself through frequent shopping sprees, is causing problems, continuing it will only cause additional problems and make existing problems worse. So, do something else instead. Find different ways of enjoying yourself! If you hear yourself saying negative things like, "I can't stay out of stores," then immediately follow such talk with, "I can't, . . . Whoops, there I go again. I can't, therefore I must!" The end of financial worries and feelings of insecurity means taking back your power. Taking your power back means changing what you are doing, and changing the way you talk to yourself. Blaming yourself or others or making excuses for yourself is not going to solve your problem and will only keep you stuck.

4. Keep it simple. Before you attempt to plan your spending, track your daily spending. Keep daily track of every penny you spend for a month. At the end of the month, total your spending and put your spending in categories, such as dining out, entertainment, etc. Tracking your spending is a reality check and is an essential step in taking your power back. Start now!

5. You cannot fail if you do something. You'll just find that you did not get the results you wanted and need to find another way. By being nonjudgmental you interpret your actions only as results, rather than as successes or failures. Labeling the results of your efforts as failures represents a self-limiting and judgmental belief that can destroy your self-esteem and self-confidence. People even generalize that unsuccessful attempts to resolve a specific financial problem reflect their complete inadequacy as human beings. This success or failure, all-or-nothing orientation is often what keeps people stuck. Be alert to such self-limiting beliefs and self-talk.

The only way to fail is to not act. Everyone makes mistakes—lots of them—on their way to taking back their power and taking control of their finances. If you act, you cannot fail; you'll only find ways to do something better! When something does not work or turn out like you wanted it to, simply say, "That didn't work; what other choices do I have? What else is possible? What other approaches can I take?"

SOLUTION-FOCUSING: CREATING SOLUTIONS INSTEAD OF LOOKING FOR THEM

Create your solutions, rather than just look for them. Whenever people go looking for solutions, they end up looking for a single all-encompassing solution that will eliminate the problem entirely. It causes people to look to other people or events to rescue them from their financial problems. It also makes people very vulnerable to scams claiming to have the very magical solution they are seeking. There are no ready-made solutions hiding out there, just waiting to be discovered. Most financial problems are not resolved by any single magical step, but by a series of small steps. As a financial counselor, I frequently hear clients say, "We had a few ideas, but those ideas won't be enough to solve the problem." What they don't yet realize is that a series of small steps, each of which by itself might seem insignificant, together with other steps will soon resolve most financial problems.

Creating solutions to financial problems is a process that requires personal action. Accomplish it by identifying what you are already doing that is positive, useful or workable. It is easier to continue what you're already doing successfully than to start doing something new. It takes far more effort to move a revolving door that is at a standstill than to continue one already in motion. Focus on what you are doing that is working, rather than what is not, and build on it. Note those times when you are managing your money effectively, so that you can do more of it. What beliefs do you have, what mental pictures or self-talk do you engage in as you motivate yourself to take action?

YOUR FEELINGS AND MONEY

Get in touch with your feelings when you find yourself spending money. Do you spend money when you are feeling lonely, angry or insecure? Do you spend to reward yourself when you've had a really great day or a bad day? Patterns and habits become deeply ingrained in our subconscious, and it becomes difficult to recognize our self-defeating behavior. Create a daily log of those times when you spend money you weren't planning to spend and your feelings at the time. Look for patterns in your behavior and in your feelings. Once you identify how you were feeling and what you have been doing to deal with those feelings, you can begin to find other, more helpful ways to feel better.

FINANCIAL TASKING: SMALL TASKS TO INITIATE ACTION

The principle of gradual improvement. Tiny refinements done daily begin to create gradual results that may be barely perceptible at first but act like magic because they are believable. Tiny refinements or changes in what you see in your mind, in the way you talk to yourself and in the actions you take, will get you unstuck. They will empower you to continue and quickly accumulate into astonishing progress.

Small steps solve large problems. Even the smallest step can become a key that unlocks the door to improving your financial situation. It initiates movement and shows you that you can influence and control events in your life. A key bite-size task is like a small stone thrown into the water. It causes ripples throughout your financial life. Tiny refinements in what you focus on in your mind, in the empowering way you begin talking to yourself and in the steps you start taking quickly become "e-motional." "E-motion" means empowering motion. Motion is empowering when you set things in motion by making slight changes in your mental focus and by imagining your life without financial fears or worries.

Motion is empowering when you hear yourself saying, "I must do it, I can do it and I am doing it even now." Motion is empowering when you act as if you already have full control of your actions. As you act with e-motion, jot down in a notebook what steps you took. Jot down how you were feeling about yourself as you took the action and *before* you become aware of any outcome, because the action itself is every bit as important as the outcome.

PRETENDING TO BE IN CONTROL OF YOUR SPENDING CREATES CONTROL

It may surprise you to know that pretending to be in control of your spending can create control. For example, in my counseling practice I have many clients who admit to having problems controlling their spending, some of whom spend money compulsively. One of the important first steps to improve their control is to complete the compulsive spending exercise I gave earlier in Chapter 4. As you'll remember, during this time I ask them to pretend that they are in control of their spending and at the end of each day to note what is happening. In almost every case, clients find that they are successfully pretending to be in control of their spending. They are astonished when I ask them, "And what meaningful distinction do you make between successfully pretending to be in control and actually being in control of your spending? If you can control your spending on the odd days of the week, one week, and on the even days of the week the next week, then you are in control. And if you were successfully pretending to be in control, then you were in control. Only if you were unsuccessfully pretending would you not be in control. Now, how does it feel to have this greater feeling of being in control than ever before?"

Start the day by pretending to be in full control of your spending. Pretend that you no longer engage in compulsive shopping and spending when you're lonely, angry or upset. Pretend that you feel both competent and confident about your financial life. At the end of the day, simply note what happens and how you're feeling, and jot it down in a few sentences in your daily log.

ELIMINATING CLUTTER

Well-chosen tasks don't even have to involve money and can become metaphors for change in financial matters. Such tasks help clarify and simplify the small steps that could also be helpful in changing financial attitudes and behavior. Each person will draw upon his or her own learning and decide the particular relevancy of metaphorical tasks. Although the following tasks do not involve money, they help people gain better control of their finances. For example, if your life is unorganized and cluttered, or if you feel overcommitted and lack free time, you probably find it difficult to organize your finances and plan for the future as well.

Eliminating clutter in our living environment—in our workplace and in our home—reduces the clutter in our minds as well. Eliminating clutter in our living environment helps us find things that may have been lost. We also can be lost in our own clutter. This process helps us find ourselves and gives us a new focus. Throwing things out, giving them away to charities and reorganizing what is left is valuable and practical. When we get rid of the clutter in our environment, we also get rid of the clutter in our lives. This creates a space in our lives that we can fill with a new focus, with our dreams and goals, and with a new sense of where we want to be and how to get there.

Eliminating clutter means getting rid of things you do not use or need, to discover things you do use and do need. Eliminating clutter also means reorganizing what you have so that you can find it and use it whenever you want to. The elimination of clutter means gaining more control of your space. Gaining more control of your space means more control of your life. By eliminating clutter you lighten up, straighten up and open up your life to new possibilities.

Organizing important household papers is an important step in eliminating such clutter, so is cleaning out your garage, basement or attic. Then, conduct a garage sale of unwanted and unused household items found in this process. By involving the entire family, everyone will cooperate more fully and pull together in dealing with your financial situation as you generate some additional cash. A garage sale can also become a useful task for getting rid of emotional baggage that may be hampering you from gaining control of your finances:

- On the left side of a large piece of paper, list the negative emotions you are feeling about your financial situation, that is, specific fears, worries, insecurities, angers, etc.

- On the right side of the page, list unwanted household items you want to sell, give to charity or throw out.

- As you sell, give to charity or throw out each item, draw a line through it on the page and one negative emotion, and say to yourself, "This is some more baggage that I do not need and have gotten rid of."

HARVESTING THE FRUITS OF YOUR LABOR

For some people, gardening is a very useful metaphor for their financial lives. Specific steps of planning the garden, including determining what to plant in the available space, planting the seeds, watering and weeding the garden regularly, all relate directly to planning our use of money. In financial planning, we determine how much money will be earmarked for specific purposes that are important to us and our families, get rid of the weeds in our spending that waste our resources and protect our "financial harvest" with the right kinds and amounts of insurance. Finally, we harvest the fruits of our financial labors in the same way that we harvest our garden, with some of it to be enjoyed now and some of it to be set aside and saved for future planting and harvesting. People who enjoy and are experienced gardeners would not think of consuming all of their harvest now, without any concern for future consumption. So it is with the financial gardener, who thinks about putting something aside so that it can be enjoyed over and over again in the future.

Cutting back vegetation and cropping certain plants foster more beautiful and luxuriant new growth than would occur if the plants were allowed to run wild. People who feel overcommitted, overwhelmed or a lack of time will begin to notice similarities between trimming their plants and trimming wasteful and expensive activities.

These are just a few of the techniques you can use to make progress on your road to financial progress and peace of mind. Above all else, remember what Bill Thompson said, "Cleaning up your finances can be fun, instead of a chore." As you think of other creative ways to gain a more secure financial life, make it a game and enjoy what you're doing. In this way, you will soon find that new, effective financial habits have become simple and regular parts of your daily life.

6.

INCREASING YOUR
CASH FLOW

Most people believe that they have already done everything possible to improve their financial situations. They typically rely on ideas or solutions to problems that may have worked in the past but are no longer effective. However, when you can identify additional choices or options, you'll develop more confidence that you are in control of your financial life and deal more effectively with any difficult financial situation that arises.

One way to create more choices in your life is by brainstorming by yourself or with your spouse to find as many new solutions and resources as possible. As you brainstorm, focus on getting as many ideas as possible, regardless of how awkward, illogical or difficult they might seem at first. Do not discuss or attempt to evaluate each idea until after you have rapidly identified as many ideas as possible! Otherwise, you will waste considerable time and end up with very few ideas. When I assist clients in doing this, we first focus our attention on identifying potential sources of additional income. I ask questions to identify the clients' resourcefulness and untapped skills that could also be used to generate income. Then we focus our creativity on ways to reduce expenses. The most frequently found additions to income and ways to reduce expenses are described in this chapter.

POTENTIAL SOURCES OF ADDITIONAL INCOME

First, you need to find the resources that will help you with your financial situation. Tax adjustments and reduced income taxes in paychecks are very helpful if you are struggling with bills, repaying creditors, meeting financial emergencies or buying badly needed insurance. There are several significant ways of adjusting your income tax to provide additional money in your paycheck.

1. Adjusting Income Tax Withholding

Change the withholding exemption on your W-4 form so that at tax time you do not owe any taxes and will get nothing back. Submit a new W-4 withholding form to your employer to do this. For example, if you received a tax refund of $900, divide this by 12 months to get the amount of your tax overpayment each month. In this example, it would be $75 overpayment withheld from each monthly paycheck. If you are in the 28 percent tax bracket, by taking one more withholding exemption you would have $59 more in your take-home pay each month. You could then use this money to reduce your debts or to save. If you received a tax refund of $1,500, you would have overpaid your federal income tax by $125 each month. This year you could take two more withholding exemptions giving you $59 × 2 = $118 more each month in your paycheck.

On your W-4 withholding form, you can claim as many exemptions as necessary to make your yearly tax obligation equal zero. For example, even if there are only four persons in your family, you can claim as many as six or eight exemptions to reduce your year-end federal tax obligation to nothing.

Another simple way of deciding the number of additional withholding exemptions to claim is as follows (based on 1996 tax tables):

1. Divide your tax refund amount in this way:
   - $380 if you're in the 15% tax bracket =
   - $710 if you're in the 28% tax bracket =
   - $790 if you're in the 31% tax bracket =
   - $920 if you're in the 36% tax bracket =
   - $1,010 if you're in the 39.6% tax bracket =

Figure 6.1　Individual Income Tax-Rate Levels

These are the tax rates for 1995 and level of taxable income in which they apply.

	15%	28%	31%	36%	39.6%
Single	up to $24,000	$24,000-58,150	$58,150-121,300	$121,300-263,700	$263,750 and over
Married, filing jointly	up to $40,100	$40,100-96,900	$96,900-147,700	$147,700-263,700	$263,750 and over
Married, filing separately	up to $20,050	$20,050-48,450	$48,450-73,850	$73,850-131,875	$131,875 and over
Head of household	up to $32,150	$32,150-83,050	$83,050-134,500	$134,500-263,750	$263,750 and over

2. You may increase your present withholding by this *additional* number of exemptions, dropping any decimal numbers (i.e., 3.3 = three more exemptions).

3. When you change the number of exemptions on your W-4 form with your employer, *each additional exemption* will increase your monthly pay by these amounts:

   • $32 if you're in the 15% tax bracket

   • $59 if you're in the 28% tax bracket

   • $66 if you're in the 31% tax bracket

   • $77 if you're in the 36% tax bracket

   • $84 if you're in the 39.6% tax bracket

   Example. Mary Smith is waiting to receive a tax refund this year of $1,200. By checking with the current year's tax tables (similar to the one I've used), she sees that she is in the 28 percent tax bracket. Dividing her tax refund of $1,200 by $710 equals 1.7 additional exemptions that she can claim on her W-4 withholding form. However, she cannot claim a partial .7 withholding exemption. By claiming one more exemption, she will receive an additional $59 each month in her monthly paycheck and still not have to pay any tax when she files her income taxes next year. Since she hasn't seen this $59 in her paycheck anyway, she decides she won't miss it if she has this automatically deposited in an IRA retirement account. If she had made this decision after several months in the year had already passed and if she badly needed this money for repaying pressing debt or for a financial emergency, she could have simply rounded the 1.7 additional withholding exemptions to 2 when she filled out a new W-4 withholding form with her employer. This would have given her an additional $118 ($59 × 2) each month to deal with this immediate emergency. However, next January she would need to drop one exemption if she didn't want to owe a little on her income the following tax year.

What surprised Mary most, however, was that she previously thought she was already claiming as many withholding exemptions as possible. There were two in her household, and she was claiming two exemptions. She didn't realize that the number of exemptions that one can legally take is not determined just by the number of people in the household.

This assumes that your financial situation this year is like last year's, that is, no big increases in household income from a spouse going to work or other windfall. On the other hand, you could increase your withholding allowances even more if during the year you had additional children or bought a house. If your spouse has become unemployed with little or no severance pay and does not expect to return to work soon, then increase the number of your federal and state withholding tax exemptions right away. By increasing the number of exemptions on the federal W-4 tax withholding form, a working spouse will have additional take-home pay until the unemployed spouse can find another job.

2. Part-Year Withholding

Persons working just part of the year (no more than 245 days, or about eight months), such as those starting a first job after graduation, may make a written request to their employer to base tax withholding on the amount actually earned during the year rather than on monthly salary. Some employers may object to this because their computer calculates the tax withholding on an annualized basis but may make an exception for you. For example, someone beginning employment on June 1st, earning $2,000 per month, is taxed on an annualized basis as though he had earned this $2,000 throughout the entire year. He would pay tax on $2,000 per month multiplied by 12 months or $24,000. Under part-year withholding, this person can ask his em-

Figure 6.2 Comparison of Earned Income Tax Credit

	Credit rate	Maximum creditable earnings	Maximum credit	Earnings for start of phase-out	Phase-out rate	Income cut-off
1996						
Families with 1 child	34.00%	$6,330	$2,152	$11,610	15.98%	$25,100
Families with 2 or more children	40.00%	$8,890	$3,556	$11,610	21.06%	$28,500
Workers without children*	7.65%	$4,220	$ 323	$ 5,280	7.65%	$ 9,500

*Must be over age 24 and under age 65.

ployer to withhold taxes based on an actual income of only $12,000 this year ($2,000 per month × 6 months), and he would be taxed at a lower rate.

3. The Earned Income Tax Credit

The Earned Income Tax Credit (EITC) is a tax credit for lower and moderate income people that varies by earnings and family size. Currently, a family with two or more children will receive an EITC equal to 40 percent of its earnings up to $8,890. See Figure 6.2 for current EITC benefits.

The EITC is a refundable credit. This means that eligible working families can benefit from the credit even if they owe no federal income tax or have no income tax withheld from their paychecks. Eligible families who owe no income tax receive a check from the IRS for their credit. If a family does owe some income tax, the EITC reduces the owed tax amount. If the family's credit is greater than the amount of taxes it owes, it reduces the family's tax bill to zero. The IRS will send the family a check for the remaining amount of its EITC benefits. EITC payments do not count as income in deciding eligibility or benefit levels for public assistance.

Retroactive EITC payments. Eligible families also may file for past EITC payments for the previous three years if they have not already done so. This could result in a significant windfall for families who may not have been filing for these benefits. A simple way to find out if you have been receiving EITC benefits is by examining the federal income tax form you have used. If you have children and have filed the shortest 1040 EZ federal tax form, then you have not been getting these benefits. By filing an amended return you could receive a small windfall of past due benefits for the past three years.

Families with a foster child or grandchildren in their homes. Low- and moderate-income working families may claim EITC benefits for a foster child living with them, if the foster child has lived with them for the entire year. Grandparents may claim EITC benefits for grandchildren living with them if the grandparents have been employed during the year. The parents of these children cannot also claim EITC benefits.

To receive EITC benefits, families must file a federal income tax return. They may use either form 1040 or 1040A. They also must file a form called "Schedule EITC" with their income tax return unless they are filing as a worker without children. Families that use the "married couple filing separately" filing status may not receive the EITC, nor if they use the 1040 EZ Form. To make filing easier, families can choose to fill out the first side of "Schedule EITC" and the IRS will calculate the amount of their EITC for them.

Advanced payment option. Eligible persons also have another option. If they are currently employed, they can receive the basic EITC benefits throughout the year in their paychecks. For example, people eligible for the maximum basic EITC benefit can have up to $101 added to their monthly paychecks. They can receive additional benefits when they file their income tax returns. Employees who wish to receive the EITC in their paychecks can ask their employer or the IRS for a W-5 form. After they complete this form and give it to their employer, the employer is then required to add the employee's EITC benefits into the employee's paychecks throughout the year.

4. The IRS Compromise Program for Taxes Owed

Occasionally, people have unpaid tax obligations that they cannot pay. The IRS has made significant changes in procedures offering a compromise of a tax debt for persons with incomes less than $100,000 and owing less than $100,000. The basis of these new and sometimes more lenient procedures is a recognition by the IRS that it is important to get people back on its tax roles. Also, that it is better to get some taxes paid on delinquent taxes than nothing. This revised program now makes a compromise easier to arrange with taxpayers who can prove hardships or circumstances that make it impossible to pay their tax obligations in full.

In a reported instance by the nonprofit Consumer Credit Counseling Service (CCCS), a client's consumer debt was $42,585, and she owed the IRS $17,016 in back taxes, penalties and interest. The counselor calculated that creditors could be paid 2% of their balances and the IRS nothing, or she could pay the creditors nothing and the IRS all that she had. If she took the latter, she would only pay part of the interest and penalties that had accrued and continue to sink deeper in debt. With the help of this resourceful credit counselor, a compromise was made using Form 656, "Offer in Compromise," Form 433A, "Collection Information Statement" and Form 2848, "Power of Attorney." The counselor mailed these completed forms to the IRS with $4,900 and later sent another $2,600 to the IRS as a final tax payment. Provided the client filed her tax returns on time for the next five years and paid any money owed on time, the IRS would keep any tax refund the following year and would forgive $9,516 of her debt. However, the amount of the offer that will be acceptable by the IRS must equal the sum of almost all of your current assets and future income over the next five years. In other words, they will not accept anything less than your minimum worth.

OTHER KEY SOURCES OF OVERLOOKED INCOME

So far we have focused on ways of finding additional sources of income from income taxes. These ways were presented first because I have found that such income tax adjustments result in additional income for about half of my clients' seeking financial counseling. In addition to income tax adjustments when seeking additional income, there are a number of other key sources of income that are often overlooked by people.

Sell assets such as stocks, bonds or property. Sometimes clients are facing dire financial situations while holding onto stocks, bonds or property that could be sold to generate additional income. This most often happens because people allow sentiment to interfere with an objective appraisal of the actual value of such stocks, bonds or property. For example, Mr. and Mrs. Dexter were faced with an unexpected series of financial circumstances with "everything coming down on them at the same time." Yet, Mr. Dexter had inherited land from his grandfather that had grown in value. He wanted to hold onto it for sentimental reasons. Mrs. Dexter had inherited stocks from her parents which had not done very well in years relative to the market, but she hadn't really looked into doing anything with them. In fact, she had no idea of their current value. Despite their dire financial situation and the mounting worry it caused, they had let their sentiment rule their good judgment. Fortunately, common sense finally prevailed, and they saw their dire financial situation as a learning opportunity to get their financial life straightened out "once and for all" as they put it.

Sell unused or seldom-used personal items, such as boats, cycles, cars, guns, recreational vehicles or other items through classified ads or a garage sale. These "toys" and other unused or outdated household items can produce badly needed cash to deal with a financial emergency. They can always be replaced when financial circumstances improve. However, most of my clients have reported that while they were initially reluctant to sell such items, they later found that they really didn't want to replace them at all, or if they did replace them, it was with something totally different. So much for their importance!

Request overtime, a raise or a job with more responsibility. While it is understandable why people are often reluctant to seek an improvement in their salary or wages in an age of job instability, difficult financial circumstances make it necessary to become more resourceful. Part of this resourcefulness is to become assertive in respect to one's own salary or wages. Even if you are turned down, just asking for a raise, overtime or a job with more responsibility will empower you, make you feel better about yourself and give you important clues about your future with your current employer. Some of my clients have decided that doing so was an eye-opener. It made them reappraise their skills in relation to their employer's plans for the future. As a result, many have gone back to school to increase their skills or to prepare themselves for a career change, or were motivated to begin seeking other, more promising employment.

Earn money from a hobby or skill. One of the most productive sources of additional income that I have found with my clients has been in helping them identify hobbies or skills that could be used to produce additional income. As a counselor, I am continually astonished at the extraordinary skills and hobbies many of my clients have that they could use to generate additional income. Many of these people are quite modest about their skills and hobbies. They have simply thought of enjoying what they do rather than making money from their hobbies or skills. In one instance, I gave a talk to a group of workers who had been laid off from their jobs with an oil company. All of these men and women were worried about how they were going to survive. During my presentation, I mentioned the importance of polishing hobbies and skills that might have become a little rusty from lack of use and building a business around them. During the break, a man rushed up to me and said, "Dr. Waddell, what you were saying was so true. My hobby is weight lifting. When I was laid off a few months ago, I went to several of the local gyms and asked if they could use a part-time weight-lifting instructor. Several of them hired me part-time, and soon I was employed with a half-dozen weight-lifting gyms. Finally, one of the gyms asked me to become their regular full-time weight-lifting instructor, and I am twice as happy now than when I was working with the oil company." I see similar scenarios occurring again and again with people who are suddenly forced to become very creative and resourceful when they have their backs up against a financial wall.

Find temporary employment for others in the household. Others in your household may be willing to find temporary employment during periods of financial hardship. Not only can this reduce the pressure and tension brought on by financial hardship, it can actually bring members of a household closer as everyone pulls together to deal with the emergency. When children who are old enough to work begin earning a part of their allowances and expenses, it teaches them self-reliance and increases their self-esteem.

Use the fifth-week system. Every third month has five paydays if you are paid weekly and every sixth month has three paydays if you are paid every other week. Use the extra money from these extra paydays to pay off installment debts or place this income into savings before it disappears into routine living expenses.

Pay off personal debts. A misuse of credit not only causes serious problems, but it also results in a considerable loss of purchasing power. The continuous use of credit consistently costs a family 20 percent more a year to live than other families who use little or no credit. By paying off his debts, a credit card user in the 28 percent tax bracket, paying 19.5 percent interest on credit cards, earns the equivalent of a huge 27 percent rate of return on his money. The average interest rate on a credit card in 1995 is about 19.5 percent, and the average amount of debt per credit card is $1,890. If your take home pay is $10 an hour, you will work about 38 hours to pay interest on this debt amount. This will not even reduce one penny of the total amount owed. Figure 6.3, on page 110, shows how many hours you must work just to pay the interest on your debt.

This table shows that the lower people's hourly take-home pay, the less debt they can afford to take on. It also shows that it is nearly impossible for people to improve their financial situations under such circumstances. This is why people with limited incomes, trying to improve their lives and gain more freedom, find instead that credit actually can erode their freedom and create more problems. If you sometimes feel that you are working harder and harder and still not getting ahead, this may be a major reason.

Zone I. If your total hours figure is located in Zone I, then you are working at least one week out of the year to pay the interest on your personal debts without reducing the amount owed.

Zone II. If the total hours figure is located in Zone II, then you are working at least one day each month (about two and a half weeks a year) to pay the interest on all of your personal debts without reducing the amount you owe.

Zone III. If the total number is located in Zone III, then you are working at least one entire month out of the year to pay the interest on all of your personal debts without reducing the amount you owe.

Zone IV. If the total number is located in Zone IV, then you are working at least one day each week (nearly two and a half months during the year) to pay the interest on all of your personal debts without reducing the amount you owe.

If you want to eliminate your credit problems, stop the loss of purchasing power and make greater financial progress, then take these steps now:

- Pay off all credit cards, revolving charges and loan balances, and increase debt repayment by increasing amounts paid on other debts as each is paid off. Use any income tax rebates, dividends or unexpected windfalls of money to pay off any credit obligations.

- On past due credit accounts, your primary goal is to reestablish a regular and reliable means of repayment. At first, do not even try to catch up with any delinquencies; they can be repaid later.

- For any credit card bill that cannot be paid off entirely at the end of the month, put that credit card away or place it in an ice cube tray, fill it with water and freeze it until that bill has been paid in full.

ARRANGING REDUCED CREDIT PAYMENTS

- Contact each creditor personally, first by phone and then with a written letter confirming any new arrangements. See Figure 6.4 for a sample letter.

- Have all the necessary papers with the account numbers in front of you (i.e., monthly statement (bill), payment booklet or credit card, delinquency notice and all prior correspondence).

- Talk to the right person (i.e., the collections manager or delinquent accounts manager). Often no one else can authorize special arrangements. Briefly explain your circumstances such as illness, job termination or other reasons for reducing your payments.

Creditors may agree to reduce payments temporarily, depending on these factors:

Figure 6.3 Working for Debt Calculator

Instructions: Simply match your hourly wage in the far lefthand column and the credit limit listed in the top line closest to your present installment debt. This is the number of regular hours you must work to pay the interest on the debt. (Items calculated on gross or net hourly wage; interest rate estimated at 20% annually.)

TOTAL NON-MORTGAGE CREDIT BALANCE										
		I.			II.		III.			
$/hr	500	1000	1500	2000	2500	3000	3500	4000	4500	5000
4.25	24	47	71	94	118	141	165	188	212	235
5	20	40	60	80	100	120	140	160	180	200
6	17	33	50	67	83	100	117	133	150	167
7	14	29	43	57	71	86	100	114	129	143
8	13	25	38	50	63	75	88	100	113	125
9	11	22	33	44	56	67	78	89	100	111
10	10	20	30	40	50	60	70	80	90	100
11	9	18	27	36	45	55	64	73	82	91
12	8	17	25	33	42	50	58	67	75	83
13	8	15	23	31	38	46	54	62	69	77
14	7	14	21	29	36	43	50	57	64	71
15	7	13	20	27	33	40	47	53	60	67
16	6	13	19	25	31	38	44	50	56	63
17	6	12	18	24	29	35	41	47	53	59
18	6	11	17	22	28	33	39	44	50	56
19	5	11	16	21	26	32	37	42	47	53
20	5	10	15	20	25	30	35	40	45	50
21	5	10	14	19	24	29	33	38	43	48
22	5	9	14	18	23	27	32	36	41	45
23	4	9	13	17	22	26	30	35	39	43
24	4	8	13	17	21	25	29	33	38	42
25	4	8	12	16	20	24	28	32	36	40
30	3	7	10	13	17	20	23	27	30	33

The author wishes to express his appreciation to Robert W. White of the Alabama Cooperative Extension System for his assistance in developing this table.

III.						IV.				
5500	**6000**	**6500**	**7000**	**7500**	**8000**	**8500**	**9000**	**9500**	**10000**	
259	282	306	329	353	376	400	424	447	471	IV.
220	240	260	280	300	320	340	360	380	400	
183	200	217	233	250	267	283	300	317	333	
157	171	186	200	214	229	243	257	271	286	
138	150	163	175	188	200	213	225	238	250	
122	133	144	156	167	178	189	200	211	222	III.
110	120	130	140	150	160	170	180	190	200	
100	109	118	127	136	145	155	164	173	182	
92	100	108	117	125	133	142	150	158	167	
85	92	100	108	115	123	131	138	146	154	
79	86	93	100	107	114	121	129	136	143	
73	80	87	93	100	107	113	120	127	133	
69	75	81	88	94	100	106	113	119	125	II.
65	71	76	82	88	94	100	106	112	118	
61	67	72	78	83	89	94	100	106	111	
58	63	68	74	79	84	89	95	100	105	
55	60	65	70	75	80	85	90	95	100	
52	57	62	67	71	76	81	86	90	95	
50	55	59	64	68	73	77	82	86	91	
48	52	57	61	65	70	74	78	83	87	
46	50	54	58	63	67	71	75	79	83	I.
44	48	52	56	60	64	68	72	76	80	
37	40	43	47	50	53	57	60	63	67	

I.

- *Whether or not the account is current.* If the account is current (not yet in arrears) creditors will usually be more willing to reduce payments temporarily. If you are one payment late, they will be less willing; if two payments behind, less so; if three payments behind, even less willing.

- *Your payment history with them.* How often have you missed payments, or how much difficulty have they had in the past collecting from you? How often have you ignored phone calls or letters requesting payment or broken past promises?

- *How tactful and honest you are.* Explain why you cannot make the scheduled payments right now. Avoid saying that the payment must have gotten lost in the mail or similar excuses. Creditors hear these excuses constantly and usually do not believe them.

Know exactly what you can afford to pay before you call. In addition, creditors may be more willing to accept the new smaller payments if you agree to a pay off plan and agree to cut up and return the credit card (close and pay off the account). Also, remember:

- You must prove that you are willing to make and faithfully carry out any new, temporarily reduced payments.

- Ask your creditors to report the new payments to the credit bureau as being on time. This will prevent these new payments from being recorded as late because they are less than the amount agreed upon in the original agreement.

- Put the agreed upon details in writing. When making the payment, include "as per our agreement on (give a date)."

- Automobile loan policies allow creditors to repossess your car with no advance notice when you are late on payments, have no auto insurance or if the car is not properly maintained, even though you're caught up on your payments. You will then have to pay the entire balance on the loan and also towing and storage costs to get it back. Before you become late on your car payments, contact the lender or car dealer as soon as possible. It may even be better to sell the car and pay off the car loan, to avoid the costs of repossession and a negative entry on your credit report.

Figure 6.4 Sample Letter

First, phone the creditor about past due payments that are likely to continue, then send a letter that includes the following information:

Your address
Date

ATTN: Name of the person you spoke with
Position title of the person you spoke with
Credit Department
Name of Company
Street or P.O. Box
City or Town, State, Zip Code

Dear Mr. (Ms.) _____ :

Thank you for speaking with me today about the problems I am temporarily having in making the payments on my account *(Give your account number here)* and for agreeing to accept *($ amount of the new smaller payment)* on my account.

As we agreed, I will make these payments on or before *(date the payments are due each month)* until *(date when full payments must be resumed or until account is paid off).*

As we agreed, I would appreciate it if you report these new arrangements to the credit bureau so that they will record these payments as being on time.

(If the creditor has asked for the return of your credit card or has closed your account, add):

I understand that you will close this account. Enclosed is my credit card that has been cut in half. Thank you again for your understanding.

Sincerely yours,

Your Signature
Your Name

RESTRUCTURE YOUR DEBTS BY REFINANCING

When trying to dig yourself out from under a heavy amount of debt, it may be necessary to restructure your debts by refinancing them. This is done by using a low interest rate loan to pay off a much higher interest rate loan. Consolidating and paying off several high interest rate loans with a much lower interest rate also can lead to just one smaller monthly payment, but spread out over a longer period of time. For example, you might want to get a low interest home equity loan to pay off all of your credit cards and revolving charge accounts.

However, exercise extreme caution when choosing this alternative. You cannot borrow yourself out of debt. There are several dangers in trying to use loans as solutions to credit problems. First, it creates an illusion of being debt-free and entices you to continue spending and using credit, which caused the debt problems in the first place. Using loans to try to deal with debt problems will usually make matters worse and create additional problems. Debt problems are like a heart attack, a clear warning that if you continue doing what you've been doing, the next round of problems could be financially disastrous. However, despite the dangers mentioned, if you decide that a loan is necessary to deal with a severe, unexpected financial emergency, then follow these important guidelines:

First, the loan should be enough to cover only the most serious emergencies. A consolidation loan to reduce your total monthly debt repayments should be just enough to deal with an emergency or with a creditor who is threatening immediate legal action. Consider these loan sources first: borrowing the cash value from a whole life insurance policy, obtaining a second mortgage or home equity loan or obtaining a loan based on some other collateral.

Second, you must be willing to put all of your credit cards on ice and not even attempt to get any other credit source until you have paid off this loan and restored your ability to pay all of your bills on time. If you find yourself slipping into old habits again, your problem may be more chronic than you think. This temporary "Band-Aid" is not going to deal with some of the deeper issues that you may not be acknowledging. If that is the case, you may want to consider seeing a financial counselor. You cannot borrow yourself out of debt! Consolidating your debts just to allow for lower, more manageable monthly payments can sometimes be useful but is always potentially dangerous. If you continue doing what you've been doing with credit, you're going to continue to get what you've been getting, only the next time, your credit problems will be much more severe and result in bankruptcy, employment problems and marital problems, just to name a few.

Once your personal debt has been paid, the monthly credit payment can then be reapplied to paying off your mortgage or to saving for retirement. Furthermore, in the event of a job loss or other financial emergency, you avoid the prospect of having creditors and debt collection agencies harassing you for payment. When paying off your debt, use the "Power Pay" principle: as you pay off each debt, apply the payment for that debt towards your other debts to pay them off much faster.

SECOND MORTGAGE AND HOME EQUITY LOANS

Home equity or second mortgage loans can be used to deal with severe financial emergencies and to pay off or reduce monthly payments on high interest credit card debts and loans. Interest on home equity or second mortgage loans is tax deductible, unlike other consumer loans. A home equity loan is an open line of credit on the existing equity in your home. A second mortgage is a single loan of a fixed amount on the equity and is a much safer option for someone who has excessive debt and uncontrolled spending. Exercise extreme caution here. If you continue to spend and to use credit as you did before the home equity or second mortgage loan, you'll be in an even deeper credit hole and could even lose your home. Since rates vary, it would be worthwhile to compare second mortgage and home equity rates at several banks and other financial institutions.

The equity in your house can sometimes be used to pay the closing costs on a home equity loan, if you cannot afford them. Also, your house equity can sometimes help you to qualify for such refinancing if your debt-to-income ratio does not qualify for such refinancing. In both cases you may need the help of a mortgage loan broker to find a financial institution willing to do this.

REDUCE YOUR LIVING EXPENSES BY STREAMLINING YOUR INSURANCE

The average person works about one month out of the year just to pay for all of the different kinds of insurance they have. A significant way to reduce any financial deficit is by examining and streamlining your insurance expenditures. Most people can reduce their insurance costs—sometimes considerably—and remain just as well insured by eliminating costly duplication, by comparison shopping and by following these seven key suggestions:

1. Avoid duplicate health insurance coverage when you and your spouse both work and cover each other. Usually, you cannot collect double payments on a claim, because insurance companies coordinate benefit payments.

2. Buy term insurance and use the savings to buy disability insurance or add to other insurance coverage.

3. Raise the deductible on your car and homeowner's insurance to equal one week's take-home pay.

4. Drop the collision and comprehensive part of your auto insurance when your car is worth $1,500 or less.

5. Shop for new auto and homeowner's insurance rates at three to four different companies.

6. Take advantage of all available discounts on auto and homeowner's insurance, by combining them at one company and by asking for safe driving, good student and safety lock, antiburglary and fire device credits.

7. Avoid purchasing or cancel the following kinds of insurance because of their high costs compared with the benefits they provide:

   - Air travel

   - Credit card

   - Dread-disease medical policies, such as cancer insurance

   - Service contracts on appliances and cars

TRACKING YOUR SPENDING: A REALITY CHECK

Keeping track of all of your spending for 30 days is part of your Money Mastery Plan and more than anything else helps you to remain financially sound. You will find that keeping track of your spending acts as a reality check. This will reveal subconscious spending habits that keep you from having things that are really important to you and from gaining better financial control and that create worry and stress. Keeping track is much easier to do than it may seem. Just follow these simple guides:

First: Ask for and save receipts for all your purchases. In those cases where receipts are not available, such as purchases through vending machines, jot down each on a slip of paper and take it with you.

Second: Establish a place to record your spending each day. The simplest way is to record it in your appointment calendar, if you already have one. If you do not have one, you can purchase a pocket size week-at-a-glance appointment calendar for a few dollars. This appointment calendar will give you enough space to record each day's spending. After each item you record, note what the expenditure was for.*

Third: At the end of the week, look back over your spending and put it into categories. In the appendix of this book is a very detailed spending plan form that will help you identify different spending categories. You do not have to use these particular spending categories. Choose categories that reflect your own spending habits and keep them simple, yet detailed enough to provide you with significant insights. For example, you may want to have several categories for food costs: groceries, carryout and fast food, vending machine food and beverages and perhaps dining out occasionally. At the end of the week, simply put each item of spending in a category that you have chosen and total the spending in that category for the week. Then add the totals for all of your spending categories. It's that simple.

---

*A good system to follow can be found in *The Money Tracker* by Judy Lawrence (Dearborn Financial Publishing, 1996).

Fourth: At the end of the month, total your spending in each category. Then, add the totals for all of your spending categories for the month. Take a good look at where you have been spending your money. Do you find anything interesting? Anything surprising? Most people quickly see that they are habitually spending money on certain things at the expense of other things that they want much more. I've provided an example of this in the story and exercise that follows:

I once had a client whose first statement was that he did not see how anyone could help him. He had no debts to speak of; the expenses he had were normal living costs and a truck payment. That was the problem. He had been making payments for several months but always for the previous month. He just could not catch up. The dealer was telling him now that he had just two months to get his payments up to date or his truck would be repossessed. He was in construction and needed his vehicle or he would lose his job. The payment was $91 per month. As we reviewed his living costs, he came to the category entitled, "food away from home." He said that he did not like fast foods and never had anything during the day.

After I asked a few questions, he finally admitted that he bought coffee every day. He was buying four cups of coffee at $.75 a cup ($3 a day) seven days a week ($3 a day times 30 days = $90 a month). When I showed him how much money he was spending on coffee, his mouth fell open. The interview was over and he left to buy a coffee-maker and a thermos. He called the next month to say that his truck payment was current for the first time in almost a year. He also said that he made a pretty fair cup of coffee. He had no idea that he was drinking his truck payments.

Exercise: What Important Financial Goal Are You Sipping or Nibbling Away Each Month?

Consider the following steps for determining how much income you might be able to save each month:

1. List all of your expenses, including any food, beverages or vending machine items that are small or inexpensive and that you buy almost daily.

2. Then figure what you spend on each of these items each week, month and during the entire year.

3. Next, think of a bill that you are behind on or have not paid or of something that you have wanted very much but felt that you could not afford.

4. Would giving up one or more of those things you have identified allow you to pay an unpaid bill or have something that you have wanted very much and felt that you could not afford?

5. Write here your own plan to pay a particular bill or to get something you want by eliminating some small expense. Include when you expect to start and when you will have achieved it. Then sign it as your personal commitment to yourself.

Expense   **Date I'll Start**   **Date I'll Achieve My Goal**

_____

_____

_____

My Signature and Date:

_____

By keeping track of your spending for a month, you can adjust your spending to provide some money for an emergency fund, to pay off your creditors more quickly or to start saving for an important goal. You can also discover how to avoid certain spending habits that may have caused you problems and prevented you from gaining better financial control. In short, keeping track of your spending will empower you to take better control of your financial life.

7.

YOUR FUTURE DEPENDS ON THE CHOICES YOU MAKE NOW

SAVINGS MADE EASY

Two nonprofit groups, Public Agenda and the Employee Benefit Research Institute, recently interviewed 1,100 people at random, including 450 government, business and academic leaders.* They conducted 16 focus groups with people throughout the country. They found that many Americans lack the knowledge, motivation and self-discipline to make sound financial decisions for themselves and their families, particularly decisions and plans for retirement. A typical comment heard was, "Between the day care, the mortgage and the car payments, we're barely able to take care of today's financial responsibilities." Another person said, "When you start saving a little bit it seems like something comes up. The car needs repairing or something else, and suddenly the savings is gone."

Most people have high expectations for their retirement and are confident they will succeed in saving enough money for it. But many of them have not yet begun to do so and sadly will wait until it's too late. Financial counselors find a growing number of older Americans in or near retirement, mired in debt and seeking debt counseling with little or no money set aside for retirement. Although Americans say they accept responsibility for their own retirement, 20 percent have

---

*Steve Farkas and Jean Johnson, *Promises to Keep: How Leaders and the Public Respond to Saving and Retirement,* a report from Public Agenda in collaboration with the Employee Benefit Research Institute, New York, 1994.

absolutely nothing saved for it, and another 13 percent have less than $10,000 put away. Twenty-three percent of people making between $40,000 and $60,000 have less than $10,000 saved. So-called strugglers, about 25 percent of Americans, have trouble keeping their heads above financial water, despite having average to higher incomes.

A recent national study by the U.S. Labor Department found that Americans don't change from being *net borrowers* to *net savers* until 44 years of age. In other words, most people aren't saving more than they are borrowing until then, and this includes saving for retirement. This average age has risen from 40 years old in the past 10 years. This has serious consequences for people's retirement plans, because it limits the powerful effect of compounding on savings and investments (compounding will be explained later).

A typical case I had exemplifies how people with the best of intentions can end up facing a bleak future. Brad and Christine Straits came to see me reluctantly. Mr. Straits, age 60, was about to become one of the thousands of middle-level managers caught up in his company's planned downsizing. His wife had been working as a secretary for a construction company. They were concerned that he was about to be laid off, and her job was also unstable. Neither of them had pension (defined benefit) plans, but their companies did have 401(k) (defined contribution) plans. The problem was that the Straits had always operated on a first-things-first philosophy. First was the purchase of a home and a decent lifestyle for themselves and their children. This was important to them because they were both from families with very limited means and remembered childhoods where deprivation was the norm. They were bonded together by a strong belief that their own children would never know such deprivation as they had experienced.

Their first-things-first philosophy then led them to concentrate on saving enough money for their two children's educations. Christine went back to work, and all savings were focused on their children's educations. By the time that their youngest child had finished college, Mr. Straits was 54 and Mrs. Straits was 50 years of age. They then turned their attention to retirement. They had begun saving money in their 401(k) plans only when their last child had graduated just six years before, thinking that with both of them working they had enough time left to begin thinking about their own retirement plans. Remembering their childhoods, they put money into their 401(k) in the most conservative fixed savings available, believing that by then they were too old to start taking any risks. They rationalized that they both had another 12 years or so of working life to earn more retirement income. When Brad was laid off, he was given a severance of one-half year's pay minus taxes so that he ended up with four months of take-home pay. A year later, Christine also was laid off from her job. Between the two of them, they had about $80,000 for their retirement years. At age 60, Brad had a life expectancy of another 25 years, and Christine about 30 years. It is essential that people begin saving and investing earlier, even if in small amounts.

EMERGENCY SAVINGS

Financial emergencies are a way of life. While we may not be able to predict exactly what kind of financial emergency will occur each year, as long as we have financial responsibilities, financial emergencies—sometimes very severe ones—are going to happen. Not having a savings fund for emergencies can be very costly and very worrisome. For example, total job security is fast becoming a thing of the past. During our work life, almost everyone will be laid off at least once, and some people today have been laid off three or four times. A recent national study has shown that it requires between five and six weeks of searching for every $10,000 you earn in income to find another job (according to a study by Drake, Beam & Morin Inc.). If you have a salary of $20,000, it would take you about 12 weeks to find another job; for a $30,000 salary, 20 weeks; for a $40,000 salary, 24 weeks; and for a $50,000 salary, 30 weeks to find another job.

Even if you receive severance pay, you need to use your savings to pay for the period without an income. The amount of your emergency savings fund should be one and a half month's take-home pay for every $10,000 in salary. Thus, someone with a $20,000 salary would need three month's take-home pay; someone with a $30,000 salary, four to five month's take-home pay; $40,000, six month's take-home pay, and a $50,000 salary, seven to eight month's take-home pay in an emergency fund. Remember that this emergency fund has to cover *all* emergencies.

However, while some rainy-day money is a must, how much you need depends on your age, health, job outlook and borrowing power in an emergency. When planning the amount of your emergency fund, consider the following:

- **Your debt load.** If you have little or no debt, you don't need as much in an emergency fund. If you have little or no mortgage debt, you'll need even less. On the other hand, if you have credit card debt and loans outstanding, home equity loans or other debts, you'll need more.

- **The stability of your income.** If your income fluctuates or is unpredictable because it is seasonal or depends on commissions, you need to adjust your savings to cover yourself during low money making periods.

- **Your job security.** Be careful here! As mentioned before, most people have been laid off at least once, and some people three and four times. If this is even a possibility and if you have no working spouse, you need to have a larger emergency fund.

- **The likelihood of a long-term disability or illness.** Consider your family's history of genetic or inherited illness as well as high-risk work or hobbies. Then examine your insurance coverage to make sure your policy is up-to-date and inclusive.

- **The possibility of a large expense such as your parents' nursing home care, or other family emergencies.** Plan for the worst case scenario so that you'll avoid unpleasant financial surprises.

Layer your emergency fund by placing some money in a short-term bond fund yielding around 6 percent, some in a mortgage prepayment plan and the rest in a mutual fund portfolio. If a severe financial emergency occurs, you can borrow from the increased equity in your home mortgage with a home equity loan or against the money you have in your mutual funds.

FINANCIAL SECURITY IN RETIREMENT MADE EASY

Warnings from financial planners that most people will need at least $1 million to retire comfortably are grossly exaggerated and only serve to frighten people who conclude that, since this is impossible, why even try! On the other hand, people's excuses that they can't afford to save or don't have the self-discipline to save, ignore the severe consequences of not saving.

You can have enough money for a financially comfortable retirement without working yourself into an early grave and without depriving yourself of a fulfilling life. If you earn $25,000 annually, social security will replace about 40 percent of your earnings. However, at higher income levels, social security replaces far less income, just 28 percent if your average annual earnings are $40,000 and only 20 percent if you earn $60,000. You will need to replace between 70 percent to 80 percent of your before-retirement income from various sources.

However, you can close this gap without becoming a workaholic or an obsessive saver. When you are older, your children's education costs are paid, your insurance needs are reduced, discount plans for seniors are available, and you have more time to do things yourself rather than rely on expensive services provided by others. Therefore, most older people can live very comfortably on 70 percent or less of what their income was in their peak earning years. By following these suggestions, you can prepare yourself for your retirement years.

CONTRIBUTE TO EMPLOYER-SPONSORED 401(K) AND 403(B) PLANS

One out of four Americans today is not taking advantage of the best savings and investment alternative available for fear of "locking up" money. Employer-sponsored 401(k) or 403(b) plans allow you to save up to $9,500 per year from your gross income and are fully tax deductible. Your employer contributes a certain amount of money to your 401(k) or 403(b) plan as well. There are also catch-up provisions that allow people with 15 years of service with a company to contribute as much as 20 percent up to $12,500 annually. A $15,000 lifetime cap applies to cumulative catch-up contributions over the $9,500.

Your money is not locked up in these plans. Most plans will allow you to borrow from them for medical emergencies, home purchases, college tuition and other serious financial emergencies. However, such borrowing should be done only as a last resort.

PAY OFF YOUR MORTGAGE EARLY

Paying off your mortgage early is a very important means of retirement planning. Not only can it become a key means of saving for retirement, money saved in this way is flexible. A home equity loan can be used to deal with a financial emergency or to help pay for a child's college education. Also, if you become unemployed, your mortgage holder may be more willing to make temporary adjustments or other concessions in your monthly mortgage payment. Money saved in this way is tax-deferred and earns interest at the same rate as your mortgage interest rate. In other words, prepaying a 9 percent mortgage is the same as earning 9 percent interest on this prepayment. It can be done by an automatic payroll deduction paid directly to the mortgage company. Note how much money is saved in the table of examples shown in Figure 7.1.

House payments usually consume 25 percent to 30 percent of a family's pretax income, so no longer having to make house payments considerably reduces the amount of money you will need in retirement. Also, if you sell the house and move to a smaller one after you're 55 years old, the first $125,000 of profit is tax-free. Even though you lose an important tax deduction when your mortgage is paid off, plan your prepayments so that your mortgage will be paid off by the time you retire. Some people prefer to make a small additional payment with each monthly mortgage payment. Others prefer to make additional payments yearly and use any windfall or extra income for this purpose.

Figure 7.1 Savings by Prepaying a Mortgage

Extra Paid Per Month	Mortgage Dollars Interest Rate & Number of Years	Shorten Mortgage by Number of Years	Interest Saved
$ 100	$75,000 10%, 30-year	12 years	$78,000
25	$75,000 10%, 30-year	5 years	34,000
100	$75,000 7%, 30-year	3 years	10,505
62*	$75,000 10%, 30-year	10 years	60,000
65.59**	$75,000 10%, 30-year	10 years	63,000

*$62 = two more withholding exemptions @ $31 each in the 15% bracket
**$65.59 = one withholding exemption in the 31% bracket

PLANNING FOR RETIREMENT ON JUST A DOLLAR A DAY

Ask yourself these questions about your retirement:

- "Is a safe, secure and comfortable retirement something I really want? Do I want it as much as some trinket I might buy?"

- "How do I look as I see myself in retirement? Am I enjoying life?"

If you are not regularly saving for retirement, you probably have no mental picture of yourself in retirement at all, let alone a picture of yourself financially comfortable and secure. Make a mental picture of yourself in retirement now. If you aren't regularly saving and investing for it, notice how bleak it is (in black and white rather than in color) or how fuzzy or hazy your picture is, with no movement and no sound to it. Get the picture? What you are seeing now in your mind is exactly what you'll be seeing later in your life, unless you begin regularly saving and investing for your retirement. On the other hand, people who are good at long-range financial goal setting and planning have mental pictures of their financial futures right in front of their eyes, and their pictures are clear, detailed and in focus.

If you are one of those people who have trouble planning, make a picture of your financial future. Then bring this picture of your financial future up close, right in front of you, and make your picture clearer, more detailed and more in focus. This will help you more clearly see what is preventing you from long-range financial planning and what you need to do.

USING INCOME TAX REFUNDS FOR RETIREMENT PLANNING

About 70 percent of people who file income taxes each year get tax refunds. The average refund in 1995 was about $1,177. Even though this windfall is nothing more than an overpayment of their income taxes throughout the year, some people won't adjust their W-4 federal income tax forms or apply for advanced Earned Income Tax Credit (EITC) because they like getting an income tax refund each year at tax time. This makes as much sense as overpaying phone bills every month just to get this extra money back a year later without interest.

As I've mentioned before, people do this because they mistakenly believe that their federal income tax is a one-time obligation that comes due every April, and that they win if they get a refund and lose if they owe money to the IRS. People also overpay on their income taxes each month because they think that they can't save money any other way, and see this overpayment and tax refund of their own money at tax time as a means of forced savings.

Rarely is the income tax refund used to purchase life, health or auto insurance, to get needed dental or medical care, or saved or invested. Income tax refunds are usually spent on things that people think they cannot live without. Studies show that this money most often is used to buy things such as cars and appliances.

Figure 7.2 shows the average income tax refund received by Americans from 1985 to 1995. It shows how much money recipients would have available for their retirement if they had just put this income tax refund during these ten years into a retirement fund. The table also shows how much of a monthly annuity they would draw from this for 25 years during their retirement. If they were to continue depositing

Figure 7.2   Using Income Tax Refund for Retirement*

Year	Average $ Refund	Years To Retire	@ 8%	@ 10%	@ 12%
1985	$ 888	35	$ 13,129	$ 24,955	$ 46,886
1986	920	34	12,595	23,504	43,321
1987	922	33	11,687	21,414	38,808
1988	897	32	10,528	18,939	33,711
1989	881	31	9,574	17,217	29,562
1990	916	30	9,217	15,984	27,443
1991	970	29	9,038	15,387	25,947
1992	1,020	28	8,800	14,709	24,362
1993	1,013	27	8,092	13,280	21,602
1994	1,069	26	7,907	12,741	24,259
1995	1,177	25	8,061	12,752	20,009
Totals	$10,673		$108,628	$190,882	$335,960
Monthly Annuity for 25 Years			$ 838	$ 1,735	$ 3,538

*Assume that you began at age 30 for next ten years. If you continued depositing a federal income tax return of $1,200 a year until age 65, you would have the following amounts saved and the following monthly annuities for 25 years of retirement:

 8% = $188,746 total; monthly annuity = $1,457
10% = $297,078 total; monthly annuity = $2,700
12% = $477,746 total; monthly annuity = $5,032

their income tax refunds of $1,200 each year for another 24 years, until they retire at age 65, they would have retirement savings and a considerable monthly annuity.

By adjusting the tax withheld (W-4) form to include one or two more federal and state exemptions throughout the year, additional money is available in each paycheck to pay off credit balances each month and earn the equivalent of a whopping 27 percent. This simple adjustment in your income tax withholding is a less expensive way to have what you want.

THE POWER OF COMPOUNDING INTEREST ON SAVINGS

You can begin planning for a more secure future and finding better ways to save and invest. This is better than giving your money to the IRS to hold for a year and then return it to you without any interest. You'll find that there are better means of forced savings than overpaying your income taxes each month. There are many kinds of automatic payroll deductions for savings and investments, where your money can grow at a rate of 6 percent or more.

Figure 7.3 shows how much a very small amount of money saved regularly each month in an automatic savings plan can grow when compounded over many years. Simply by changing your W-4 form to add just one more exemption so that slightly less is withheld from your monthly paychecks can provide a secure retirement when this money is saved and compounded over many years.

For example, for people in the lowest 15 percent tax bracket, each additional withholding exemption means an additional $32 dollars a month ($380 a year). By changing their W-4 withholding form to claim just one additional withholding exemption and arranging an automatic payroll deduction (a more sensible means of forced saving than over-withholding on income taxes), and by investing this $32 in an IRA or other retirement plan, in 30 years they will have accumulated $111,839, and $376,472 in 40 years.

For people in the middle income 28 percent tax bracket, each additional exemption provides $59 more per month or $710 per year. In 30 years, people in this tax bracket will have accumulated $206,203, and $694,121 in 40 years.

For people in the 31 percent tax bracket, each additional withholding exemption provides $66 more per month or $790 per year. In 30 years they will have accumulated $230,668, and $776,475 in 40 years.

For people in the 36 percent tax bracket, each additional withholding exemption provides $77 more per month or $920 per year. In 30 years they will have accumulated $269,112, and $905,888 in 40 years. By adding two more exemptions during the year, you can double the above retirement savings.

Figure 7.3   Effect of Withholding Exemptions on Retirement

One additional withholding exemption for persons in:		
15% Tax Bracket		
Dollars Invested Each Month	$32	$32
Number of Years	30	40
Future Value at 12% Interest	$111,839	$376,472
28% Tax Bracket		
Dollars Invested Each Month	$59	$59
Number of Years	30	40
Future Value at 12% Interest	$206,203	$694,121
31% Tax Bracket		
Dollars Invested Each Month	$66	$66
Number of Years	30	40
Future Value at 12% Interest	$230,668	$776,475
36% Tax Bracket		
Dollars Invested Each Month	$77	$77
Number of Years	30	40
Future Value at 12% Interest	$269,112	$905,888

RETIREMENT ON JUST A DOLLAR A DAY

Because of the powerful effect of compounding on savings over many years, this small change in withholding not only will enable you to pay off your home sooner and provide money for your retirement, but also provide the peace of mind, sense of security and self-confidence that comes from knowing that you are taking care of your financial well-being. Notice that this can be achieved with virtually no sacrifice. The yearly amount set aside in an IRA or other retirement investment is far below the $2,000 that can be placed into a tax-free IRA each year. Also, earnings from money put into an IRA or other retirement plan are tax deferred and for many people may be tax deductible.

Because of the magic of compounding, these amounts combined with Social Security retirement benefits can enable you to live comfortably in retirement. This can be done even if you begin saving just a dollar a day when you are 25 years old until retirement at age 65. Even if you begin saving a dollar a day when you are 35 years old, you still can be financially secure in retirement.

However, the longer you procrastinate, the more you deprive yourself of the magic of compounding and a financially secure retirement. If you do not begin saving for retirement until you are 45 years old and plan to retire at age 65, even this amount over just 20 years can be helpful. Procrastination is very costly to our financial security. Waiting until just 10 years before retirement greatly limits the powerful effects of compounding (see Figure 7.4). Then you must greatly increase the amount of money you save if you are going to enjoy a financially secure future.

OTHER TIPS

- If you plan to keep working when you retire, even on a reduced schedule, there is much less reason to pile up money now. For many people, this may mean investing in developing new skills in addition to savings. Many people find their new jobs after retirement even more satisfying than the jobs they held before retiring. However, most of these people have planned for and prepared themselves for these retirement jobs before they retire. Improve your skills in other work areas that you intend to pursue or in income-producing hobbies that you enjoy. Develop plans for marketing yourself and your services and products.

- Save any money you inherit. If you are lucky enough to receive a small inheritance, remember that you got it because your relatives acted sensibly instead of adding to their pile of material stuff. Follow their wise example.

- Also, a modest cabin in the country may turn out to be a better long-term investment than other kinds of investment. And if you rent it out to friends, family and coworkers occasionally, you may be able to buy it without sacrificing much.

- Last but not least, create a close network of family and friends. A supportive group of loved ones leads to many rewards both personally and professionally. You'll be grateful for such a network which can be a great source of contentment and happiness during retirement.

Figure 7.4   How Time Affects the Value of Money

Investor A invests $2,000 a year for 10 years, beginning at age 25. Investor B waits 10 years, then invests $2,000 a year for 31 years. Compare the total contributions and the total value at retirement of the two investors.

Investor A				Investor B			
Age	Year	Contribution	Year-End Value	Age	Year	Contribution	Year-End Value
25	1	$2,000	$ 2,188	25	1	$ 0	$ 0
26	2	2,000	4,580	26	2	0	0
27	3	2,000	7,198	27	3	0	0
28	4	2,000	10,061	28	4	0	0
29	5	2,000	13,192	29	5	0	0
30	6	2,000	16,617	30	6	0	0
31	7	2,000	20,363	31	7	0	0
32	8	2,000	24,461	32	8	0	0
33	9	2,000	28,944	33	9	0	0
34	10	2,000	33,846	34	10	0	0
35	11	0	37,021	35	11	$ 2,000	$ 2,188
40	16	0	57,963	40	16	10,000	16,617
45	21	0	90,752	45	21	10,000	39,209
50	26	0	142,089	50	26	10,000	74,580
55	31	0	222,466	55	31	10,000	129,961
60	36	0	348,311	60	36	10,000	216,670
65	41	0	545,344	65	41	10,000	352,427
Value at Retirement			$545,344	Value at Retirement			$352,427
Less Total Contribution			(20,000)	Less Total Contribution			(62,000)
Net Earnings			**$525,344**	**Net Earnings**			**$290,427**

Note: Assume a 9 percent fixed rate of return, compounded monthly. All interest is left in the account to allow interest to be compounded.

POSTPONING PROCRASTINATION

We have seen just how costly procrastination can be. People who live only for today, saying they will worry about tomorrow when it comes, find that this becomes a self-fulfilling prophecy later.

People procrastinate because they have concerns and fears about their daily survival needs, or because their perfectionist attitudes block them from taking action. Typical excuses and rationalizations that interfere with financial planning include: "I live one day at a time," "Whatever will be, will be," "My only financial concern is how to pay the bills," "I live from hand to mouth." If you use any of these excuses, you probably have a problem with procrastination.

Some people think that they must first take care of certain financial responsibilities before dealing with others. One-thing-at-a-time thinking only leads to costly procrastination. Usually, we have to take care of several responsibilities at the same time. We don't say, "I'll wait until my children are grown before I give to my church," or "I'll wait until I have completed paying for my house before saving for a vacation or for my children's education." Just a little now can make a huge difference. Instead of thinking in terms of an either-or use of your money, think in terms of a little of both: a little spent on something I want now, *and* a little spent on something later, a secure retirement and peace of mind.

The following exercise will help you to determine more clearly the consequences of procrastination in financial matters:

Close your eyes for a moment. Now imagine that you have been retired for one year; for five years; for ten years. As you see yourself now, or perhaps you and your spouse in these pictures, what do you see? How do you and your spouse look? Happy? Confident? Carefree and with peace of mind? If these are not the pictures you see, what do you see? How do you and your spouse look? Now, imagine yourself in your 70s working at a local fast-food hamburger place. Can you see yourself with that little cap on your head, working with kids young enough to be your grandchildren? Just how do you feel as you see yourself in this scene. Are you happy with this picture? Is this what you want retirement to look like for you, sound like feel like? If not, then isn't it time to do something about it now?

If you tend to procrastinate but want to change your old habits, you can start by asking yourself the following questions:

1. "What goals have I set for myself in other areas of my life that I accomplished?"

_____

_____

_____

2. "What plans have I made that turned out well?"

_____

_____

_____

3. "What do I need to do now to change things for myself?"

_____

_____

_____

4. "Instead of living hand to mouth, how would I like to live?"

_____

_____

_____

5. "What has stopped me? What would I need to do for this to no longer stop me?"

_____

_____

_____

THE CURSE OF PERFECTIONISM

Another reason for procrastinating in planning or in taking action might be based on an underlying fear that a financial decision might not be perfect, best or right. People who have this fear can be heard saying, "Unless I can devote the time to do this 'right,' I won't do it at all." Or they will say, "I'm not going to attempt it unless you can guarantee me that . . ." These statements merely reflect their underlying perfectionism and the fear that feeds it. Many financial problems result from perfectionism. The more one procrastinates about financial matters, the more difficult it is to stop procrastinating and to take action. If you tend to be a perfectionist, think about this:

- Human beings are never perfect, and you are human.

- Therefore, the only thing that you can do perfectly is to allow yourself to be less than perfect.

- Rather than pursue impossible perfection, pursue a possible goal instead.

The Powerful "P" Principles of Procrastination

Perfectionism only produces *procrastination,* and *procrastination* is *progressive* and produces *profoundly powerless people.* On the other hand, *purpose, persistence* and *patience* produce empowering *progress.*

Compounding is just as significant when applied to our actions. Small steps quickly compound into new, productive beliefs and habits that soon lead to dramatic results. On the other hand, avoidance, inaction and procrastination compound rapidly into overwhelming feelings of powerlessness and helplessness. Take action to ensure yourself a secure future right now. You'll be grateful you did.

8.

IF YOU SLIP

How often do we read or hear stories about people who came to this country as poor immigrants and yet retire as millionaires? These stories are true, and the details of these stories offer encouragement to us all. As you read about these people, you find common threads running through all of their stories. Most of them began working in minimum wage jobs that no one else wanted. Even then, these people managed to save a few dollars. As their jobs and incomes improved, the savings habits that they had formed enabled them to save and invest even more. In other words, even on very meager incomes, they were able to put some of their money to work for them. Every one of these people later claimed that they didn't miss the money that they had saved, and that this money had helped them to survive the inevitable financial storms that blew from time to time, and to prosper.

Our ability to ride out financial storms without drowning, and our ability to bounce back quickly from such storms, depends on our having a safety cushion of savings, and the habits we have developed become our rudder that keeps us on course to a safe port. Our savings enable us to bounce back quickly when unexpected financial blows have knocked us down. Reading this book will not shield you from any financial storms, but the new habits that you develop and put into use will enable you to weather such storms and to find a safe port more easily and quickly.

As a financial counselor, I can most often help people regain their financial stability and improve their financial control considerably after just two counseling sessions. Success is determined when three things happen:

1. At least a small but significant change has occurred in respect to goals or desired outcomes.

2. The change that appears is durable; it will last.

3. Clients feel they can handle things themselves.

By no means do I imply that their financial problems will disappear and never again reappear. However, they now have the knowledge, skills and confidence to deal with any financial storms that may occur from time to time. This depends as much on what they do after they leave my office as what occurs while in my office. After leaving my office, its time to get behind the wheel and point their financial vehicle in a new direction. In short, it's time to act on this information and use these new skills to do something! Confidence is built by actually doing something, not just by thinking about it.

In the same manner, just reading this book—or any book—or attending a financial seminar, regardless of how good it is, will do nothing for your financial life unless you actually do something with the new knowledge and skills that you have acquired.

In addition, I sometimes receive phone calls from clients several weeks or several months later, claiming that they have slipped back into old ineffective attitudes and habits. When this happens, they are completely focused on the fact that they have slipped or made mistakes in some way, and that the knowledge, skills and new habits they had acquired have somehow failed them. In responding, I ask them several questions:

- "How long has it been since we worked together on your problem?"

- "What if I had developed a pill that when taken would automatically give you exceptional money-management knowledge, skills and confidence that would take care of any financial problem for several months, but you would need to take another booster pill every couple of months? Would you consider such a pill successful, even a major scientific achievement?"

- "So, you have been doing quite well for a couple of months now but have recently slipped in a few respects. Is it time for your booster?

Okay then, I want to give you your booster by simply asking you some questions":

- "Were the times that you slipped back into old ineffective habits fewer than before? Are the mistakes fewer than ever before?"
- "How did you manage to get yourself back on track again?"
- "What do you need to do now to get yourself back on track?"
- "How do you plan to do this?"

Instead of focusing on the brief time of their mistakes, people need to remember the considerable amount of time when they manage quite well. Then they need to focus on what they did to get themselves back on track. This more appropriate focus is, in fact, the very booster pill they need to stop "catastrophizing" about any mistakes and get on with what they were doing so well for so long.

So it will be for you as you begin relying more and more on your new beliefs, habits, greater self-esteem and confidence to guide you back to your safe port, despite any problem that might arise.

For parents, there is another extraordinary by-product of your new skills and self-confidence. You will have given your children one of the greatest gifts that loving parents can give to their children, the gift of resourceful, confident role models who are in control and who don't use money like a narcotic to deal with life's ups and downs, parents who walk their talk with financial balance and inner peace throughout their lives.

I suggest that one month from now, you go back to the six self-assessments in Chapter 10. Do the self-assessments again to see for yourself what has changed in your mind and in your life. You will notice even more changes in the days, weeks and months to come.

Now, I don't know if you have realized it yet, but the more you look for those old ways of reacting to money matters, the more they seem to disappear. In fact, the more you try to find those old reactions to money, the faster they disappear. So what you need to do now is take a few moments and try harder and harder to find any of those old reactions to money matters. Notice how they have disappeared faster and more completely, or simply just disappear each day as you try again, until you realize that you have already changed. When you have realized that, I want you to think of your future and try in vain to experience those old reactions to money matters, because the more you try, the more you will automatically respond in the new confident ways. And the more you try to react in those old ways, the more the new responses automatically occur, and with surprising results.

I'm wondering just how surprised will you be when you and significant other people in your life begin noticing the new, more powerful you, feeling and acting with more confidence and feeling better about yourself than ever before?

Just do it, and notice that soon you're enjoying the process and having fun!

9.

Epilogue: Metamorphosis

Once upon a time, a caterpillar found itself slowly inching its way across the earth, its tiny legs clinging and clutching closely to the ground beneath it in order to feel safe and secure. It looked up in the sky, saw a butterfly and said, "You'll never catch me in one of those things!"

It seemed to take forever to move such a little distance, and the little caterpillar wondered, "Why? What's the use?" Yet, it felt pulled by some unseen force, sensing that somehow there must be some purpose to it all, and that there must be a way to stop feeling so vulnerable to predators and to being accidentally harmed by other beings and events.

So the caterpillar slowly inched its way up a tree and out onto a limb to see a little better. As it reached the end of the limb, it said, "I'm beat; this has been a lot of work. I've been struggling and struggling for nothing. I feel at the end of my limb (as the saying goes)." And the little caterpillar began to spin a safe, secure and protective cocoon around itself, as caterpillars are prone to do.

Once inside that cocoon, though, a miracle happened. Soon, the little caterpillar began to feel confined, stifled and uncomfortable. It finally decided that it had to get out of there and struggled to get free. As it did, it wondered, "Is this what life is all about, just one struggle after another?" And it struggled and struggled, pulling and pushing this way and that, until it finally got one little leg up, a second leg up and then its head. When it saw the bright sunlight, so very different from the darkness inside the cocoon, it was even more eager to be free of that stifling cocoon. As the caterpillar emerged into the warm inviting sunlight, it was delightfully surprised to find that it had been transformed into a beautiful butterfly, with wings that allowed it to catch the wind and to soar higher and higher.

Now, high above the earth, it looked back at the cocoon that once held it safely and protectively but had become too confining and smothering. It now saw its old, seemingly protective cocoon in a new way. In fact, it saw the world itself in a much different way than ever before. A world that used to seem so very confusing and frightening, now seemed so much clearer and safer from this new perspective. The butterfly started to feel very proud of itself and of the new things it saw and could do now.

As it looked down from its new perspective above, it noticed another little caterpillar on the ground below, looking up in amazement, negatively shaking its little head. And the butterfly, remembering such a time before, shouted to the caterpillar, **"Yes, you can! Yes, you will! It's only a matter of time! For you see, your own metamorphosis is inevitable, because you already have everything you need inside you to make it happen . . . just do it!"**

PART TWO

PUTTING THE MONEY MASTERY PLAN TO WORK FOR YOU

10.

DEVELOPING YOUR MONEY MASTERY PLAN

If you ask people how they think they are doing financially, most will answer with something like, "Oh, I'm probably doing as well as the next person." But people typically don't know how well the next person is or is not doing, nor do they have any kind of objective way of determining just how well they themselves are doing financially. I often see clients who have no idea of their financial condition and sometimes do not even want to believe an experienced financial counselor's assessment either. For these reasons, I have developed a series of simple self-assessments that clients can use to determine their own "financial health." These self-assessments have either been validated through research by the author or other financial scholars, or they have considerable face-validity from my experience with clients over the years and from reports of other financial counselors during my counselor training sessions. Also, while no one test by itself is a completely accurate picture of someone's financial condition, when taken together the assessments provide a very accurate picture of a person's financial condition.

As you do these self-assessments simply relax. No one needs to see the results but you. The assessments are not intended to judge or find fault, but only to enlighten you by pinpointing possible problem areas that either could use improvement or that may be obstacles to your success and to guide you in dealing with such problems. So find yourself a quiet place, get a pen or pencil, and have fun!

Another complete set of self-assessments is included that you or your spouse can use later to reassess personal progress.

Let's begin the process of money mastery by completing the following six self-assessments that you can use to determine your own financial health. You are the only one who needs to see these self-assessments, and they are provided only to increase your self-awareness. These self-assessments will reconfirm for you, areas where you are financially on track and pinpoint other areas where you are possibly having problems. They also will help you identify specific money management practices that are causing problems and interfering with your money mastery.

Self-Assessment One:
Typical Concerns That People Reveal about Money

Self-assessment one will help you identify typical concerns and worries people have about money that can be eliminated with this money mastery program.

Self-Assessment Two: Profile of My Financial Health

Self-assessment two will help you identify specific financial problems or harmful habits with money that can be resolved with this program. It also enables you to rate your own financial health.

Self-Assessment Three: Debt Level Risk

Self-assessment three will help you assess the degree of risk your debts pose relative to your income. The degree of risk posed by your debts will help you assess how vulnerable you are to any financial emergency and to possible insolvency and bankruptcy. The higher the percentage, the more overextended you are with credit and the more vulnerable you are to financial crises and bankruptcy.

Self-Assessment Four: Severity Level of Financial Problems

Self-assessment four will enable you to determine the severity level of any financial problems. By circling the numbers beside each statement that may apply to you, you will be able to quickly see how serious any financial problems are and identify specific money management practices that must be addressed.

Self-Assessment Five: Financial Control Profile

Self-assessment five provides 21 statements to determine how much control you have of your financial life. These statements also represent 21 sound money management attitudes and habits that, if followed, will ensure your financial health and happiness throughout your life. They provide an excellent list of desirable lifetime financial outcomes.

Self-Assessment Six: Spending Out of Control

Self-assessment six provides 13 statements to determine how much control you have over your spending. From this assessment you can determine if you are a normal spender, recreational spender, borderline spender, compulsive spender or addicted spender.

SELF - ASSESSMENT ONE

Typical Concerns That People Reveal about Money

Instructions: Check the ones that are your concerns.

	1. I worry about money and my financial future.		13. I don't deserve financial success or can't have it even if I deserve it.
	2. I am embarrassed or feel guilty about my financial life.		14. I'd rather not know about my financial condition.
	3. I argue about money with family members.		15. I often feel I'd better get what I want right now, because I may not be able to get it later.
	4. I don't want to know about my financial condition.		16. I'm afraid of becoming financially independent
	5. I get upset when talking about money.		17. I'm hoping that someday, someone will rescue me from my financial problems.
	6. I am not responsible for my financial future.		18. You can't plan your spending and at the same time be spontaneous.
	7. I put off making financial decisions or taking any action.		19. My financial situation is not my fault or my responsibility.
	8. I feel my spending gets out of control sometimes.		20. I will become too materialistic and sacrifice my spirituality if I plan and control my use of money.
	9. I can't budget or plan my spending.		**SCORING:** There is no scoring in this self-assessment. Instead, just note statements that you have checked which reflect your own problems or concerns so that they can be eliminated with this money mastery program.
	10. I have trouble saving money.		
	11. If I'm too successful I may lose my friends.		
	12. If I succeed, then failure is probably just around the corner.		

SELF - ASSESSMENT TWO
Profile of My Financial Health

Instructions: For an understanding of your financial health,
respond Y (Yes) or N (No) to each of the following statements.

	1. A creditor is taking legal action against me.		11. I do not have automobile insurance.
	2. One or more of my creditors is threatening to take legal action against me.		12. I am behind on one or more of my credit installment payments.
	3. Part of my wages or salary is deducted to pay a wage assignment or garnishment.		13. I am being turned down for a loan or other credit.
	4. I am receiving past-due notices on my charges or bills.		14. I am charging up to the limit on one or more credit cards.
	5. I take out new loans to pay off old ones.		15. I am paying only the minimum amount due each month on one or more credit cards.
	6. In order to pay my rent, utility or grocery bills, I have to skip installment payments or take out loans.		16. I rely on the automatic-loan overdraft protection of my checking account.
	7. I am behind on my rent.		17. Items and services that I used to buy with cash, I now buy on credit.
	8. I am behind on my utility bills.		
	9. I am considering filing for bankruptcy.		18. In order to pay current bills, I have sold non-matured bonds or stocks.
	10. I do not have health insurance.		19. I do not know how much I owe on all my outstanding debts combined.

Continued on the Following Page

20. I do not know how much my total monthly payments are on all my debts combined.	23. My monthly mortgage (or rent) plus utilities is more than 50 percent of my take home pay (net income)
21. Members of my household and I argue about money.	24. To pay bills, I withdraw money from savings.
22. I worry about money and money problems.	25. I have less than one month's net income in savings or other liquid assets.

Scoring and Interpretation	
1. Score 3 points for each Yes answer on questions 1–11 =	points
2. Score 2 points for each Yes answer on questions 12–22 =	points
3. Score 1 point for each Yes answer on questions 23–25 =	points
ADD YOUR SCORE HERE:	points

0>>>>>>>>>>>>>>>>>>13>>>>>>>>>>>>>>>>>>>>26>>>>>>>>>>>>>>>>>>>>>58

Financial problems or concerns: Corrective action important.	**Serious problems:** Immediate corrective action important. Financial counseling suggested.	**Severe to very severe problems:** Immediate corrective action and financial counseling essential.

SELF - ASSESSMENT THREE
Debt Risk

Total Monthly Credit Payments To Total Monthly Net Income

1.	List and total the required monthly payments on all loans (including education and automobile loans) and credit cards, but *not* monthly mortgage payments. = $	**Debt Signals**
2.	List and total all of your net monthly income (take-home pay). Net monthly income is your gross income minus all required/standard deductions, for example, income taxes,* social security, employer health and life insurance, union dues, court-ordered child support payments (if deducted from wages). = $	**Debts Without Mortgage** More than 40% — Severe debt problems certain 35% — Debt problems certain 30% — Debt problems likely 25% — Debt problems may occur 20% — Safe limit for debt (Debt to net income) Less than 20% **Debts Without Mortgage**
3.	Divide #1 $ _____ by #2 $ _____ = _____ % (move decimal two places to right). This is your total monthly debts payment *(without mortgage payment)* as a proportion of monthly take-home pay. (See note below.)	**Debts With Mortgage** More than 60% — Severe debt problems certain 55% — Debt problems certain 50% — Debt problems likely 45% — Debt problems may occur 40% — Safe limit for debt (Debt to net income) Less than 40% **Debts With Mortgage**
4.	Use the Debt-Signals bar in *the right column* and the percentage limit for each zone to determine the risk of your current debt loan.	
	Note: You may be able to increase your take-home pay if you are eligible for the federal Earned Income Tax Credit (EITC). Call the Internal Revenue Service.	

SELF-ASSESSMENT FOUR
Severity Level of Financial Problems

Instructions: Circle the number of each statement that applies to you.

I. Moderate: I am having trouble with . . .
1. Seasonal (infrequent) bills such as insurance, taxes, membership dues, etc.
2. Routine gifts for Christmas, birthdays, anniversaries, etc.
3. Repairs of car, appliance, home, etc.
4. Lack of money for unexpected events, special needs
5. Little or no savings
6. Use of savings for routine living expenses
7. Some worry, anxiety, family arguments about money
8. Increasing balances on credit cards, charge accounts

II. Serious (financial counseling recommended): I am experiencing . . .
9. Spending 4 percent or more of my take-home pay on alcohol or nonprescribed drugs
10. Can't afford basic essentials such as food, clothing
11. No health insurance
12. No auto insurance
13. Postponement of health care need—medical, dental—for self or family
14. Some reduction in family income—money often runs out before payday
15. Frequent worry, family arguments regarding money
16. Interference in job, family duties or with relationships

III. Severe (financial counseling essential): I am experiencing . . .
17. Spending 6 percent or more of take-home pay on alcohol or nonprescribed drugs
18. Insolvency (unable to pay bills and other financial obligations when due)
19. Threatened (possible) loss of food, housing (eviction), foreclosure, utilities
20. Legal action threatened by creditors, collection agencies
21. Litigation fees from divorce, defendant in civil suit, etc.
22. Medical expenses with inadequate insurance coverage
23. Negative cash flow
24. Some reduction in family income

IV. Very Severe (financial counseling essential): I am experiencing . . .
25. Spending 6 percent or more of take-home pay on alcohol or nonprescribed drugs
26. Physical survival endangered
27. Loss of food, housing or utilities
28. Legal action by creditors in process (i.e., wage assignment, repossession, foreclosure, seizure of assets or property, etc.)
29. Filing or decision to file bankruptcy
30. Defendant in a criminal case
31. Large medical expenses with little or no insurance
32. Loss or severe reduction in family income

Note: If you are experiencing some problems in Category III (Severe), you are also likely to be experiencing many of the problems in Categories I and II as well.

SELF - ASSESSMENT FIVE
Financial Control Profile

**21 Beliefs and Practices That Indicate How Much
Control You Have of Your Financial Life**

Yes	No	Do I truly believe that:
		1. I deserve and am fully capable of achieving financial stability, progress and abundance.
		2. I take full responsibility for my financial situation and accept that I am the only one who can control it and change it.
		3. I avoid spending money in ways that might cause pain, sorrow or problems for myself or for others.
		4. I honestly assess the true state of my financial condition.
		5. I examine honestly and face squarely my attitudes, behavior and fears about money.
		6. I free myself of worry, guilt, embarrassment and depression about money matters.
		7. I determine clear and specific financial goals for my future financial well-being.
		8. I review my income and expenses occasionally to spot untapped resources, to eliminate waste, and to bring my spending, saving and investing in line with my financial goals and needs.
		9. I examine my buying habits and seek out information before spending or investing money.
		10. I accept financial emergencies as inevitable and prepare in advance for them by saving.
		11. I reward myself and my efforts and build my self-esteem, freedom and independence by saving some of my money.
		12. I develop and follow a saving and investing plan that reflects my financial goals, and a spending plan that prioritizes my needs and wants.
		13. I maintain a simple spending record and examine it periodically in order to keep my goals and my progress in sharp focus.

Continued on the Following Page

Yes	No	Do I truly believe that:
		14. I follow a debt reduction plan until all of my debts are under control.
		15. I inform myself about credit and use it cautiously.
		16. I fulfill my financial obligations to my children and educate them in these essential principles of financial maturity.
		17. I communicate with my spouse and children about money matters openly and calmly and without blaming or finding fault.
		18. I am flexible in my attitudes and expectations about money and its use when dealing with my family and others.
		19. I am aware of what is enough when it comes to material possessions and realize that more possessions do not necessarily bring happiness or peace of mind.
		20. I know how costly and addictive it is spending money to change my moods rather than to satisfy my needs and wants.
		21. I am charitable in appreciation for the many blessings I have received, and to express my self-confidence in money matters.
People who ignore these important principles suffer financial hardships throughout their lives, sometimes without knowing why. On the other hand, people who follow these principles are able to avoid major financial crises and worry, tend to be financially secure, have peace of mind and make financial progress throughout their lives.		

SELF-ASSESSMENT SIX
Spending Out of Control

Is My Spending Out of Control?

Instructions: For statements 1 to 3 below, give your response by circling one of the following: Strongly Agree (SA), Agree (A), Neutral/No Response (NR), Disagree (D) or Strongly Disagree (SD).

	SA	A	NR	D	SD
1. I feel driven to shop and spend, even when I don't have the time or the money.					
2. I get little or no pleasure from shopping.					
3. I hate to go shopping.					

Instructions: For statements 4 to 13 below, please indicate how often you engage in the following activities by circling one of the following for each activity: Never (N), Rarely (R), Sometimes (S), Often (O) or Very Often (VO).

	N	R	S	O	VO
4. I go on buying binges.					
5. I feel "high" when I go on a buying spree.					
6. I buy things even when I don't need anything.					
7. I go on a buying binge when I'm upset, disappointed, depressed or angry.					
8. I worry about my spending habits but still go out to shop and spend money.					
9. I feel anxious after I go on a buying binge.					
10. I buy things even though I cannot afford them.					
11. I feel guilty or ashamed after I go on a buying binge.					
12. I buy things I don't need or won't use.					
13. I sometimes feel compelled to go shopping.					

Source: Elizabeth A. Edwards, *The Measurement and Modeling of Compulsive Consumer Buying Behavior.* Published dissertation, the University of Michigan: University Microfilm, 1992. Scale for measuring compulsive buying behavior used with permission of author.

Scoring: Give yourself the number of points for each question as shown below.					
					Your Score for Each Question
1. SA = 4	A = 3	NR = 2	D = 1	SD = 0	
2. SA = 0	A = 1	NR = 2	D = 3	SD = 4	
3. SA = 0	A = 1	NR = 2	D = 3	SD = 4	
4. N = 0	R = 1	S = 2	O = 3	VO = 4	
5. N = 0	R = 1	S = 2	0 = 3	VO = 4	
6. N = 0	R = 1	S = 2	0 = 3	VO = 4	
7. N = 0	R = 1	S = 2	0 = 3	VO = 4	
8. N = 0	R = 1	S = 2	0 = 3	VO = 4	
9. N = 0	R = 1	S = 2	0 = 3	VO = 4	
10. N = 0	R = 1	S = 2	0 = 3	VO = 4	
11. N = 0	R = 1	S = 2	0 = 3	VO = 4	
12. N = 0	R = 1	S = 2	0 = 3	VO = 4	
13. N = 0	R = 1	S = 2	0 = 3	VO = 4	
Add Points Above for Your Total Score =					

Interpretation of Score:				
1. To get your average score for all 13 items, divide your total score by 13 = _____ 2. On the scale below find your average score.				
Normal/ Noncompulsive Spender	Recreactional Spender	Borderline Spender	Compulsive Spender	Addicted Spender
0	0.1–1.11	1.11–2.28	2.28–3.46	3.46–4.00

Determining Your Direction

Find a time and place where you can enjoy some privacy as you complete the next few pages. Use a pencil so that you can change your answers if you change your mind. There are no right or wrong answers to this process of self-discovery and self-motivation, so enjoy yourself as you begin this process.

- What is going on in your financial life that you no longer want? Or, what is *not* going on in your financial life that you want to see happening?

_____

_____

_____

_____

- How would you like for things to be different? What would you like to achieve financially? My goal is

_____

_____

_____

_____

- To identify your key goal, ask yourself three or four times, "So, what will having this (your previous answer) do or get for me that's positive?"

_____

_____

_____

_____

- "What will achieving (your previous answer) do for me?"

_____

_____

_____

_____

- If possible, identify one time when you have been able to accomplish this goal or one time when the problem that your goal addresses does _not_ occur! How did you manage to do this?

_____

_____

_____

_____

- What is something you do really well, something you take great pride in, something you know deep inside you do well, and that perhaps other people have said you do well? Describe it here!

_____

_____

_____

_____

- As you look at yourself now succeeding at this task, how do you manage to do this? Jot your answers to these questions in the space below:

  1. What do you see yourself doing?

  2. How do you plan or organize it?

3. What do you say to yourself and how do you talk to yourself to get started (not only what words do you use, but what tone of voice do you use)?

4. How do you feel as you begin?

5. What do you see in your mind to encourage yourself to keep going?

6. What do you say to yourself as you finish each step or part of it?

7. What do you say to yourself when you have finally finished?

_____

_____

_____

_____

_____

_____

• Can you think of another example? Describe it here!

_____

_____

_____

_____

• As you look at yourself now succeeding at this other task, how do you manage to do this?

1. What do you see yourself doing?

2. How do you plan or organize it?

3. What do you say to yourself and how do you talk to yourself to get started (not only what words do you use, but what tone of voice do you use)?

4. How do you feel as you begin?

5. What do you see in your mind to encourage yourself to keep going?

6. What do you say to yourself as you finish each step or part of it?

7. What do you say to yourself when you have finally finished?

_____

_____

_____

_____

_____

_____

- The beliefs, skills, self-talk and approach that you enjoy using in tasks that you do well are the same ones you can use to improve your financial situation. The resources and skills that you use in these other experiences are ones such as the following:

- Visualize the task completed.
- Say encouraging things to yourself.
- Keep a positive tone of voice.
- Break the task into parts or steps.
- Display self-confidence.
- Change fear into excitement.
- Be resourceful.
- Be creative.
- Act and follow through.
- Be persistent.
- Congratulate or reward yourself.
- Be a decision maker.
- Plan.
- Motivate yourself.
- Gather information.

1. Which of these resources and skills do you enjoy using in tasks that you do so well? Which of these resources and skills do you now see yourself using and enjoying as you deal with financial matters?

   _____

   _____

   _____

2. What new beliefs do you now have about your finances as you see yourself doing these other tasks so well?

   _____

   _____

   _____

- Identify three possible choices, options or approaches to achieving your goal!

  1. _____

  2. _____

  3. _____

- Identify three resources (including your skills and strengths) you now have that you can use to master your money!

  1. _____

  2. _____

  3. _____

- Has there been a stumbling block on the path to money mastery?
  Yes _____ No _____
  What three things would you be willing to do to prevent this stumbling block from getting in the way again?

1. _____

2. _____

3. _____

11.

DEVELOPING A SPENDING PLAN

The forms in this section can be used for entering the results of tracking your spending for a month. A spending plan emphasizes the importance of before-the-fact planning. These forms are very detailed in order to allow you to probe line items in each spending category. In Worksheet C, Spending Inventory—Monthly Expenses, use the *Before* column as an income and expense inventory to enter amounts that you are currently spending. Use the *Adjusted* column to enter whatever adjustments in spending you choose to make. The last column on the right allows you to record the plus or minus dollar differences between the *Before* and *Adjusted* columns. Surplus (+) amounts in this column can be used for debt repayment and to reduce income minus expenses deficits.

You will see that different kinds of expenses have their own form. Worksheet A, Debt Payments, and Worksheet B, Insurances and Other Seasonal Expenses, are listed first because they are usually fixed amounts; Worksheet C, Spending Inventory—Monthly Expenses, has both fixed and variable expenses; Worksheet D, Gifts, Cards, Flowers, and Worksheet E, Emergencies and Future Goals, are variable expenses. The final form is a Spending Plan Summary. Categorizing expenditures on these forms in this manner is useful in quickly determining how you are using your incomes and to ensure that periodic expenses are noted and planned for. Remember that even so-called fixed expenses can sometimes be changed if necessary. Watch out for insurance premiums and other periodic expenses that may soon be due and for which money may need to be set aside.

Identifying Income

I. Employers			
Job #1		**Job #2**	
A. Gross $	Per	A. Gross $	Per
B. Deductions/Withholdings (Total 1–9)	$	B. Deductions/Withholdings (Total 1–9)	$
1. Federal Income Tax	$	1. Federal Income Tax	$
2. State Income Tax	$	2. State Income Tax	$
3. FICA	$	3. FICA	$
4. Retirement	$	4. Retirement	$
5. Health Insurance	$	5. Health Insurance	$
6. Life Insurance	$	6. Life Insurance	$
7. Credit Union	$	7. Credit Union	$
8. Union Dues	$	8. Union Dues	$
9. Other	$	9. Other	$
C. Net (take home pay) Subtract B from A	$	C. Net (take home pay) Subtract B from A	$

II. Retirement		II. Retirement	
A. Gross	$	A. Gross	$
B. Deductions/Withholdings (Total 1–6)	$	B. Deductions/Withholdings (Total 1–6)	$
1. Federal Income Tax	$	1. Federal Income Tax	$
2. State Income Tax	$	2. State Income Tax	$
3. FICA	$	3. FICA	$
4. Insurance	$	4. Insurance	$
5. Allotments	$	5. Allotments	$
6. Survivor Benefit Plan	$	6. Survivor Benefit Plan	$
C. Net (Subtract B from A)	$	C. Net (Subtract B from A)	$
Average Gross Per Month	$	**Average Gross Per Month**	$

Rules for Converting to Monthly Amounts

If your information is in:	Adjust as shown below:
Days	$ amount $\times 365 \div 12$
Weeks	$ amount $\times 52 \div 12$
Every Two Weeks	$ amount $\times 26 \div 12$
Irregular	Work out an estimate for the year and divide by 12

WORKSHEET A
Debt Payments

All Debt Balances and Payments Except Mortgage

Instructions: Use pencil.

Creditors or Collection Agency	Purpose of Debt	Months Past Due	Remaining Balance	Monthly Payment	Plan To Pay Off by (Mo. & Yr.)
1.					
2.					
3.					
4.					
5.					
6.					
7.					
8.					
9.					
10.					
11.					
12.					
13.					
14.					
15.					
16.					
17.					
18.					
19.					
20.					
TOTALS			$	$	

WORKSHEET B
Insurances and Other Seasonal Expenses

Instructions: Use pencil.

Insurance or Seasonal Expenses	Date Needed	Prior Amount Needed by:		New Amount Needed by:		Difference Per:	
		Due Date	Year	Due Date	Year	Due Date	Year
1. Life Insurance							
2. Health Insurance							
3. Disability (Loss of Income Insurance)							
4. Auto Insurance							
5. Homeowner's Insurance (Do not include if paid with mortgage-Schedule A)							
6. Umbrella Insurance							
7. Marine (Boat)/Other Insurance							
8. Auto Tags, License Renewal							
9. Taxes							
10. Other (Specify)							
11. Other (Specify)							
12. Other (Specify)							
TOTALS		$	$	$	$	$	$

WORKSHEET C
Spending Inventory—Monthly Expenses
Instructions: Use pencil.

	Subtotal Before	Before	Adjusted	Subtotal Adjusted	+ or – $ Difference Between Before & Adjusted
1. Support Payments (Fixed)	$_____	_____ Spousal Support (Alimony) _____ _____ Child Support		$_____	$_____
2. Shelter (Fixed)	$_____	_____ Rent or Mortgage Payment _____ _____ Property Tax _____ _____ Homeowner's or Tenant Ins. _____ _____ Lot Rent _____ _____ Condominium Maintenance _____ _____ Exterminator/Pest Control _____ _____ Gardening/Yard Work _____ _____ Cable TV _____		$_____	$_____
3. Shelter Operation (Variable)	$_____	_____ Water, Sewer, Garbage _____ _____ Gas _____ _____ Electricity _____ _____ Telephone _____ _____ Furnace/AC (cleaning check) _____ _____ Home and Appliance repair _____ _____ Domestic Help _____ _____ Other _____ _____		$_____	$_____
4. Clothing (Variable)	$_____	_____ Purchase for Self _____ _____ Purchase for Spouse _____ _____ Purchase for Children _____ _____ Laundry and Dry Cleaning _____ _____ Alterations/Shoe Repair _____		$_____	$_____
5. Child Care & Education (Variable)	$_____	_____ Day Care, Nursery _____ _____ Babysitting _____ _____ Tuition and Fees _____ _____ Lessons _____ _____ School Activities _____		$_____	$_____

	Subtotal Before	Before	Adjusted	Subtotal Adjusted	+ or – $ Difference Between Before & Adjusted
6. Food (Variable)		_____ Main Grocery Trips	_____		
		_____ Emergency Grocery Trips	_____		
		_____ Co-op, Butcher, Baker			
		_____ Farmer's Market			
		_____ Coffee Breaks/Vending			
		_____ Snacks			
		_____ Lunch Out on Weekday			
		_____ Dinner Out on Weekday			
		_____ Breakfast Out			
	$_____	_____ Carryout/Fast Food		$_____	$_____
7. Transportation (Variable)		_____ Gas and Oil	_____		
		_____ Tune-ups, Lube Job	_____		
		_____ Tires	_____		
		_____ Major Repairs	_____		
		_____ Bus Fare	_____		
		_____ Cab Fare	_____		
		_____ Parking Fee/Ticket	_____		
	$_____	_____ Other _____	_____	$_____	$_____
8. Health (Variable)		_____ Hospital	_____		
		_____ General Physical	_____		
		_____ Gynecologist	_____		
		_____ Pediatrician	_____		
		_____ Other Conditions	_____		
		_____ Chiropractor	_____		
		_____ Dental	_____		
		_____ Eye Exam	_____		
		_____ Glasses	_____		
		_____ Contacts	_____		
		_____ Drugs (prscpt/nonprscpt)	_____		
		_____ Dietary Supplements	_____		
	$_____	_____ Counseling/Therapy	_____	$_____	$_____
9. Donations (Variable)		_____ Church	_____		
		_____ Charities	_____		
		_____ Political Causes	_____		
	$_____	_____ Other (specify) _____	_____	$_____	$_____

Continued on the Following Page

	Subtotal Before	Before	Adjusted	Subtotal Adjusted	+ or – $ Difference Between Before & Adjusted
10. Personal (Variable)		_____ Haircuts, Permanents _____ Cosmetics, Hair Products _____ Cigarettes _____ Organizations/Clubs _____ Professional Dues _____ Allowances _____ Pets (veterinarian)	_____ _____ _____ _____ _____ _____ _____		
	$_____	_____ Other (specify) _____	_____	$_____	$_____

11. Recreation/ Entertainment (Variable)		_____ Hobbies and Materials
		_____ Personal Development and
		    Physical Improvement
		_____ Alcohol (outside home)
		_____ Alcohol (at home)
		_____ Entertainment/Recreation
		    (specify type of)
		_____ a. _____
		_____ b. _____
		_____ c. _____
		_____ d. _____
		_____ e. _____
			_____
			_____
			
			_____
			_____
			
			_____
			_____
			_____
			_____
			_____		

	$_____	_____ f. _____	_____	$_____	$_____
12. Miscellaneous (Variable)		_____ Newspapers _____ Magazine Subscriptions _____ Magazines, Newstand _____ Records/Tapes/CDs _____ Books _____ Library Fines _____ Postage	_____ _____ _____ _____ _____ _____ _____		
	$_____	_____ Other _____	_____	$_____	$_____
Summary Worksheet C (Categories 1–12)	$_____			$_____	$_____

WORKSHEET D
Gifts, Cards, Flowers (Variable)

Instructions: Use pencil.

These items merit their own form. Most people have little idea of just how much is spent for gifts, cards and flowers every year, and these can ruin a spending plan. Estimate as accurately as possible what you will spend on gifts for each person or occasion, when the gifts will have to be purchased and the amounts to be set aside each month this year to have the necessary cash available when these occasions arise. Then, add your estimated costs for all of these gifts, cards and flowers for the year and how much you will need to set aside each month.

Occasion	Probable Cost	Date Needed	Check if Already Purchased	Amount To Set Aside This Year	Amount To Set Aside per Month
1. Mother's/ Father's Day					
2. Anniversaries					
3. Weddings					
4. Showers					
5. Graduations					
6. Baby Gifts					
7. Valentine's Day					
8. St. Patrick's Day					
9. Thanksgiving					
10. Grandparents' Day					
11. Easter/Passover					
12. Rosh Hashanah					
13. Christmas/ Chanukah (List)					
14. Birthdays (List)					
Totals				$	$

WORKSHEET E
Emergencies and Future Goals

Instructions: Use pencil.

This form is for savings and investments, for emergencies, for such things as the purchase of a house, car, household appliances, or other major purchases or purposes. This important form has been placed last to demonstrate that if all expenses on all of the other forms (A through D) are added and compared to totals of net income, little or no money may be left over for savings, emergencies, retirement, or investment and future financial growth. It emphasizes the importance of planning and saving for these important purchases and purposes first, before other expenses are paid.

Purposes for Savings and Investment Funds	Estimated Amount Needed	Adjusted Amount To Set Aside This Year	Adjusted Amount To Set Aside This Month	Type of Savings/ Investment and Institution
1. Emergencies				
2. Christmas/Chanukah				
3. Vacation (Summer)				
4. Vacation (Winter)				
5. Future Education (self)				
6. Future Education (children)				
7. New Home, Major Repair, Improvement				
8. Auto Replacement				
9. Major Appliance and Equipment Replacement				
10. Retirement				
11. Bar Mitzvah				
12. Other (specify)				
Totals			$	$

WORKSHEET F
Spending Plan Summary

Initially, this process of estimating and planning spending, saving and investing may be consuming, but it is the very heart of a spending plan and the key to gaining financial control and making financial progress.

Summary of Worksheets and Spending Categories	Total Adjusted This Year	Total Adjusted This Month	Projected Differences + or −
I. Fixed Expenses 1. Debt Payment (Worksheet A)			
2. Seasonal Expenses (Worksheet B)			
3. Emergencies/Future Goals (Worksheet E)			
4. Support Payment (Child/Spousal)			
5. Shelter			
Subtotal: Fixed Expenses			
II. Variable Expenses			
6. Shelter: Operation			
7. Clothing			
8. Child Care			
9. Food			
10. Transportation			
11. Health			
12. Donation			
13. Personal			
14. Recreation/Entertainment			
15. Miscellaneous			
16. Gifts, Cards, Flowers (Worksheet D)			
Subtotal: Variable Expenses			
Total: Fixed and Variable Expenses			$

12.

SAMPLE SPENDING PLAN

Instructions: Use the adjusted dollar amounts developed from Worksheets A to E.

I. Monthly Amount Planned for Each Expense Category	II. Category Includes:	III. Record Spending Here: Month _January_	IV. Amount Spent	V. + or – Difference Between Cols. I & II
Summary (Total) of Worksheets A–E Adjusted $2847.34	All Planned Expenses This Month	_____ _____ _____	$3,375.00	$ -530.67
Worksheet A Adjusted $125.00	Total Debt Payments Due This Month	All paid as agreed _____ _____	$ 125.00	$ 0
Worksheet B Adjusted $ 88.34	Total Insurances/Seasonal Exp. Due This Month	$110 life insurance (6 months) $440 car insurance (6 months)	$ 530.00	$ -441.67
Worksheet E Adjusted $150.00	Emergencies and Future Goals Savings This Month	$50 vacation account $25 Christmas account $50 emergency fund $25 furniture/appliance fund	$ 150.00	$ 0

Net (take-home) pay available this month $ _____ minus
Total amounts required for fixed expenses Worksheets A, B and E $ _____ equals
Total amount ($) available for variable expenses Worksheets C and D = $ _____

175

Worksheet C Planned	Category Includes:	Record Spending in This Column	Amount Spent	+ or − Difference Between Cols. I & IV
1. Support Payments (Fixed) Adjusted $250.00	Spousal Support (Alimony) ___ Child Support ___	_____ _____ _____ _____	$ 250.00	$ 0
2. Shelter (Fixed) Adjusted $575.00	Rent/Mortgage Payment ___ Property Tax *included in mortgage* Homeowner's/ Tenant's Insur. ___ Lot Rent ___ Condo Maint. ___ Exterminator/ Pest Control ___ Garden/Yard ___ Cable TV __25__	$550.00 _____ _____ _____ _____ _____ _____ _____ _____ _____ $25.00	$ 250.00	$ 0
3. Shelter Operation (Variable) Adjusted $129.00	Water/Sewer/ Garbage __15__ Gas __60__ Electricity __25__ Telephone __20__ Furnace/AC (Clean, check) __4__ Home Appl Repair. __5__ Domestic Help ___ Other ___	$15 monthly bill $70 monthly bill $30 monthly bill $25 monthly bill	$ 140.00	$ −11.00
4. Clothing (Variable) Adjusted $105.00	Purchase—Self __25__ Purchase—Spouse __25__ Purchase— Children __40__ Laundry/Cleaning __10__ Alt./Shoe Repair __5__	$60 dress, $40 shoes, $15 shirt, $40 shoes, $40 (2 pr. sneakers) $6	$ 1210.00	$ +3.00
5. Child Care/ Education (Variable) Adjusted $250.00	Day Care, Nursery __150__ Babysitting __40__ Tuition, Fees __20__ Lessons __20__ School Activities __20__	$150 $10, 10, 10, 10 $10, 10 $10 − Sue, $ − Ralph $5, 3, 3, 6	$ 247.00	$ +11.50

Worksheet C Planned	Category Includes:		Record Spending in This Column	Amount Spent	+ or – Difference Between Cols. I & IV

6. Food
(Variable)
 	
Adjusted
$485.00
	Main Grocery
	  Trip
	Emergency Groc.
	Co-op, Butcher,
	  Baker
	Farmer's Market
	Coffee Breaks/
	  Vending Mach.
	Snacks
	Lunch Out/Wkdy.
	Dinner Out/Wkdy.
	Breakfast Out
	Carryout/Fast food
		
		355
		8
		
		18
		
		10
		10
		60
		
		10
		14
			$190, 155
			$4, 7,6
			
			$14.50
			$7
			$2, 3, 1.50
			$6, 6 (See receipts)
			
			See entertainment
			$9
			$8.50
			
				$ 473.50
					
					$ +11.50

7. Transportation (Variable) Adjusted $ 80.00	Gas and Oil Tune-up, Lube Tires Major Repairs Tire Repair Bus Fare Cab Fare Parking Fee/ Ticket Other	55 10 10 	$10, 12, 9, 11 $49.50 See entertainment $9 $3.50 	 $ 95.00	 $ -105.00
8. Health (Variable) Adjusted $ 70.00	Hospital Gen. Physical Gynecologist Pediatrician Other Conditions Chiropractor Dental Eye Exam Glasses Contacts Drugs (pres./non) Diet Supplements Counsel/Therapy	 4 10 20 11 10 15 	 $40 checkup for Ralph $35 John $100 contacts – John 	 $ 175.00	 $ -105.00
9. Donations (Variable) Adjusted $ 65.00	Church Charities Political Causes	60 5 	$15, 15, 15, 15 	 $ 60.00	 $ +5.00

Worksheet C Planned	Category Includes:	Record Spending in This Column	Amount Spent	+ or – Difference Between Cols. I & IV
10. Personal (Variable) Adjusted $ 180.00	Haircuts, Perms ___50___ Cosm./Hair Prod. ___5___ Cigarettes _____ Organizations/ Clubs ___5___ Professional Dues ___20___ Allowances ___95___ Pets (vet) _____ Other (specify) _____	$15 John , $25 Mary, $10 Ralph $4 John, $1 Mary _____ _____ None due this month _____ _____ _____ $40 John, $40 Ralph, $15 Mary	$ 151.00	$ +29.00

11. Recreation/
Entertainment
 	
Adjusted
$210.00
	Hobbies and
	  Materials _____
	Personal Dvlp. ___20___
	Physical Imprvmt. ___30___
	Alcohol (away) _____
	Alcohol (home) _____
	Entertainment/
	  Recreation _____
	(specify type) _____
	
	40 a Bowling _____
	20 b Movies _____
	80 c Dinners out _____
	   d _____
	   e _____
	   f _____
		$40 Personal devlpmt seminar
		$30 Health club dues
		
		$19
		_____
		_____
		_____
		_____
		$10, 10, 10, 10 John/Mary
		$12, 12 Family
		$51 John/Mary
		_____
		_____
		_____
		_____
			$ 206.00	$ +4.00

12. Miscellaneous (Variable) Adjusted $ 35.00	Newspapers ___15___ Magazine Sub. ___5___ Magazine, Newstand ___6___ Records/Tapes/CDs _____ Books ___5___ Library Fines _____ Postage ___4___ Other _____	$15 $5 $2.50, 3.50 John _____ $8.50 Mary _____ _____ _____ _____	$ 34.50	$ +50.00
Worksheet D Adjusted $ 50.00	Gifts, Cards, Flowers Due This Month	John's birthday $44 Get well card mother $1	$ 45.00	$ +5.00
Total Spending For Worksheets C & D This Month $ _____			$2570.00	Overall + or – Difference Between Cols. I & IV $ –89.00

APPENDIX A

Additional
Self-Assessment Forms

Typical Concerns That People Reveal about Money

Check the ones that are your concerns

	1. I worry about money and my financial future.		13. I don't deserve financial success or can't have it even if I deserve it.
	2. I am embarrassed or feel guilty about my financial life.		14. I'd rather not know about my financial condition.
	3. I argue about money with family members.		15. I often feel I'd better get what I want right now, because I may not be able to get it later.
	4. I don't want to know about my financial condition.		16. I'm afraid of becoming financially independent
	5. I get upset when talking about money.		17. I'm hoping that someday, someone will rescue me from my financial problems.
	6. I am not responsible for my financial future.		18. You can't plan your spending and at the same time be spontaneous.
	7. I put off making financial decisions or taking any action.		19. My financial situation is not my fault or my responsibility.
	8. I feel my spending gets out of control sometimes.		20. I will become too materialistic and sacrifice my spirituality if I plan and control my use of money.
	9. I can't budget or plan my spending.		**SCORING:** There is no scoring in this self-assessment. Instead, just note statements that you have checked which reflect your own problems or concerns so that they can be eliminated with this money mastery program.
	10. I have trouble saving money.		
	11. If I'm too successful I may lose my friends.		
	12. If I succeed, then failure is probably just around the corner.		

Profile of My Financial Health

For an understanding of your financial health,
respond Y (Yes) or N (No) to each of the following statements.

	1. A creditor is taking legal action against me.		11. I do not have automobile insurance.
	2. One or more of my creditors is threatening to take legal action against me.		12. I am behind on one or more of my credit installment payments.
	3. Part of my wages or salary is deducted to pay a wage assignment or garnishment.		13. I am being turned down for a loan or other credit.
	4. I am receiving past-due notices on my charges or bills.		14. I am charging up to the limit on one or more credit cards.
	5. I take out new loans to pay off old ones.		15. I am paying only the minimum amount due each month on one or more credit cards.
	6. In order to pay my rent, utility or grocery bills, I have to skip installment payments or take out loans.		16. I rely on the automatic-loan overdraft protection of my checking account.
	7. I am behind on my rent.		17. Items and services that I used to buy with cash, I now buy on credit.
	8. I am behind on my utility bills.		
	9. I am considering filing for bankruptcy.		18. In order to pay current bills, I have sold non-matured bonds or stocks.
	10. I do not have health insurance.		19. I do not know how much I owe on all my outstanding debts combined.

Continued on the Following Page

	20. I do not know how much my total monthly payments are on all my debts combined.		23. My monthly mortgage (or rent) plus utilities is more than 50 percent of my take home pay (net income)
	21. Members of my household and I argue about money.		24. To pay bills, I withdraw money from savings.
	22. I worry about money and money problems.		25. I have less than one month's net income in savings or other liquid assets.

Scoring and Interpretation	
1. Score 3 points for each Yes answer on questions 1–11 =	points
2. Score 2 points for each Yes answer on questions 12–22 =	points
3. Score 1 point for each Yes answer on questions 23–25 =	points
ADD YOUR SCORE HERE:	points

0>>>>>>>>>>>>>>>>>>13>>>>>>>>>>>>>>>>>>>>>>26>>>>>>>>>>>>>>>>>>>>>>>58

Financial problems or concerns: Corrective action important.	**Serious problems:** Immediate corrective action important. Financial counseling suggested.	**Severe to very severe problems:** Immediate corrective action and financial counseling essential.

Debt Risk

Total Monthly Credit Payments To Total Monthly Net Income

1.	List and total the required monthly payments on all loans (including education and automobile loans) and credit cards, but *not* monthly mortgage payments. = $	**Debt Signals**
2.	List and total all of your net monthly income (take-home pay). Net monthly income is your gross income minus all required/standard deductions, for example, income taxes,* social security, employer health and life insurance, union dues, court-ordered child support payments (if deducted from wages). = $	**Debts Without Mortgage** — More than 40% / Severe debt problems certain; 35% / Debt problems certain; 30% / Debt problems likely; 25% / Debt problems may occur; 20% / Safe limit for debt (Debt to net income); Less than 20%. **Debts With Mortgage** — More than 60% / Severe debt problems certain; 55% / Debt problems certain; 50% / Debt problems likely; 45% / Debt problems may occur; 40% / Safe limit for debt (Debt to net income); Less than 40%. Debts Without Mortgage. Debts With Mortgage.
3.	Divide #1 $ _____ by #2 $ _____ = _____ % (move decimal two places to right). This is your total monthly debts payment *(without mortgage payment)* as a proportion of monthly take-home pay. (See note below.)	
4.	Use the Debt-Signals bar in *the right column* and the percentage limit for each zone to determine the risk of your current debt loan.	
	Note: You may be able to increase your take-home pay if you are eligible for the federal Earned Income Tax Credit (EITC). Call the Internal Revenue Service.	

Severity Level of Financial Problems

Circle the number of each statement that applies to you.

I. Moderate: I am having trouble with . . .
1. Seasonal (infrequent) bills such as insurance, taxes, membership dues, etc.
2. Routine gifts for Christmas, birthdays, anniversaries, etc.
3. Repairs of car, appliance, home, etc.
4. Lack of money for unexpected events, special needs
5. Little or no savings
6. Use of savings for routine living expenses
7. Some worry, anxiety, family arguments about money
8. Increasing balances on credit cards, charge accounts

II. Serious (financial counseling recommended): I am experiencing . . .
9. Spending 4 percent or more of my take-home pay on alcohol or nonprescribed drugs
10. Can't afford basic essentials such as food, clothing
11. No health insurance
12. No auto insurance
13. Postponement of health care need—medical, dental—for self or family
14. Some reduction in family income—money often runs out before payday
15. Frequent worry, family arguments regarding money
16. Interference in job, family duties or with relationships

III. Severe (financial counseling essential): I am experiencing . . .
17. Spending 6 percent or more of take-home pay on alcohol or nonprescribed drugs
18. Insolvency (unable to pay bills and other financial obligations when due)
19. Threatened (possible) loss of food, housing (eviction), foreclosure, utilities
20. Legal action threatened by creditors, collection agencies
21. Litigation fees from divorce, defendant in civil suit, etc.
22. Medical expenses with inadequate insurance coverage
23. Negative cash flow
24. Some reduction in family income

IV. Very Severe (financial counseling essential): I am experiencing . . .
25. Spending 6 percent or more of take-home pay on alcohol or nonprescribed drugs
26. Physical survival endangered
27. Loss of food, housing or utilities
28. Legal action by creditors in process (i.e., wage assignment, repossession, foreclosure, seizure of assets or property, etc.)
29. Filing or decision to file bankruptcy
30. Defendant in a criminal case
31. Large medical expenses with little or no insurance
32. Loss or severe reduction in family income

Note: If you are experiencing some problems in Category III (Severe), you are also likely to be experiencing many of the problems in Categories I and II as well.

Financial Control Profile

**21 Beliefs and Practices That Indicate How Much
Control You Have of Your Financial Life**

Yes	No	Do I truly believe that:
		1. I deserve and am fully capable of achieving financial stability, progress and abundance.
		2. I take full responsibility for my financial situation and accept that I am the only one who can control it and change it.
		3. I avoid spending money in ways that might cause pain, sorrow or problems for myself or for others.
		4. I honestly assess the true state of my financial condition.
		5. I examine honestly and face squarely my attitudes, behavior and fears about money.
		6. I free myself of worry, guilt, embarrassment and depression about money matters.
		7. I determine clear and specific financial goals for my future financial well-being.
		8. I review my income and expenses occasionally to spot untapped resources, to eliminate waste, and to bring my spending, saving and investing in line with my financial goals and needs.
		9. I examine my buying habits and seek out information before spending or investing money.
		10. I accept financial emergencies as inevitable and prepare in advance for them by saving.
		11. I reward myself and my efforts and build my self-esteem, freedom and independence by saving some of my money.
		12. I develop and follow a saving and investing plan that reflects my financial goals, and a spending plan that prioritizes my needs and wants.
		13. I maintain a simple spending record and examine it periodically in order to keep my goals and my progress in sharp focus.

Continued on the Following Page

Yes	No	Do I truly believe that:
		14. I follow a debt reduction plan until all of my debts are under control.
		15. I inform myself about credit and use it cautiously.
		16. I fulfill my financial obligations to my children and educate them in these essential principles of financial maturity.
		17. I communicate with my spouse and children about money matters openly and calmly and without blaming or finding fault.
		18. I am flexible in my attitudes and expectations about money and its use when dealing with my family and others.
		19. I am aware of what is enough when it comes to material possessions and realize that more possessions do not necessarily bring happiness or peace of mind.
		20. I know how costly and addictive it is spending money to change my moods rather than to satisfy my needs and wants.
		21. I am charitable in appreciation for the many blessings I have received, and to express my self-confidence in money matters.

People who ignore these important principles suffer financial hardships throughout their lives, sometimes without knowing why. On the other hand, people who follow these principles are able to avoid major financial crises and worry, tend to be financially secure, have peace of mind and make financial progress throughout their lives.

Spending Out of Control

Is My Spending Out of Control?					
Instructions: For statements 1 to 3 below, give your response by circling one of the following: Strongly Agree (SA), Agree (A), Neutral/No Response (NR), Disagree (D) or Strongly Disagree (SD).					
	SA	**A**	**NR**	**D**	**SD**
1. I feel driven to shop and spend, even when I don't have the time or the money.					
2. I get little or no pleasure from shopping.					
3. I hate to go shopping.					
Instructions: For statements 4 to 13 below, please indicate how often you engage in the following activities by circling one of the following for each activity: Never (N), Rarely (R), Sometimes (S), Often (O) or Very Often (VO).					
	N	**R**	**S**	**O**	**VO**
4. I go on buying binges.					
5. I feel "high" when I go on a buying spree.					
6. I buy things even when I don't need anything.					
7. I go on a buying binge when I'm upset, disappointed, depressed or angry.					
8. I worry about my spending habits but still go out to shop and spend money.					
9. I feel anxious after I go on a buying binge.					
10. I buy things even though I cannot afford them.					
11. I feel guilty or ashamed after I go on a buying binge.					
12. I buy things I don't need or won't use.					
13. I sometimes feel compelled to go shopping.					

Source: Elizabeth A. Edwards, *The Measurement and Modeling of Compulsive Consumer Buying Behavior.* Published dissertation, the University of Michigan: University Microfilm, 1992. Scale for measuring compulsive buying behavior used with permission of author.

Scoring: Give yourself the number of points for each question as shown below.					
					Your Score for Each Question
1. SA = 4	A = 3	NR = 2	D = 1	SD = 0	
2. SA = 0	A = 1	NR = 2	D = 3	SD = 4	
3. SA = 0	A = 1	NR = 2	D = 3	SD = 4	
4. N = 0	R = 1	S = 2	O = 3	VO = 4	
5. N = 0	R = 1	S = 2	0 = 3	VO = 4	
6. N = 0	R = 1	S = 2	0 = 3	VO = 4	
7. N = 0	R = 1	S = 2	0 = 3	VO = 4	
8. N = 0	R = 1	S = 2	0 = 3	VO = 4	
9. N = 0	R = 1	S = 2	0 = 3	VO = 4	
10. N = 0	R = 1	S = 2	0 = 3	VO = 4	
11. N = 0	R = 1	S = 2	0 = 3	VO = 4	
12. N = 0	R = 1	S = 2	0 = 3	VO = 4	
13. N = 0	R = 1	S = 2	0 = 3	VO = 4	
			Add Points Above for Your Total Score =		

Interpretation of Score:				
1. To get your average score for all 13 items, divide your total score by 13 = _____				
2. On the scale below find your average score.				
Normal/ Noncompulsive Spender	Recreactional Spender	Borderline Spender	Compulsive Spender	Addicted Spender
0	0.1–1.11	1.11–2.28	2.28–3.46	3.46–4.00

APPENDIX B

Highly Recommended References

Dominguez, Joe and Vicki Robin. *Your Money or Your Life.* 1992. *Transforming Your Relationship with Money and Achieving Financial Independence.*

A powerful book that reveals not just how to manage our finances but how to integrate our financial responsibilities with the rest of our lives. This extraordinary book deals with the essential questions of money in our lives. Are we making a living or making a dying? What is enough for us in terms of material things? Are we playing the game, "my pile (of things) is bigger than your pile (of things)"? Viking Penguin, New York ($11.00, paperback).

Lawrence, Judy. *The Money Tracker.* 1996.

A tracking guide that can be carried with you to jot down your successes and personal insights. It has a useful "splurge diary." Dearborn Financial Publishing, Inc., Chicago ($14.95, hardcover).

Roman, Sanaya and Duane Parker. *Creating Money: Keys to Abundance.* 1988.

A step-by-step guide to creating money and abundance in your life. The premise of this book is that if we follow the spiritual laws of money and abundance, develop unlimited thinking, listen to our inner guidance, visualize abundance in our lives, create our life's work and transform our beliefs, then we will magnetize and attract the abundance and prosperity that is our natural state. It teaches how to let money flow readily into our lives while doing what we love through visualization, positive affirmations and exercises. You do not have to work hard to have abundance but can learn to work with energy to easily create what you really want. Life Mastery Series - Book 1. H.J. Kramer Inc., Tiburon, Calif. ($12.95, paperback).

Waddell, Fred E. *The Debt Checker/Working for Debt Calculator* and *The Debt Signals Ruler.* 1995.

These take-along debt gauges assist you in gaining control of your finances. Use the *Debt Checker* to find your own safe limits for personal debt, comparing monthly take-home pay with total monthly non-mortgage debt to determine your credit status—from your ability to increase credit to your knowledge that you have severe credit problems. This is an essential check when preparing to make a credit purchase or just verifying where you stand. On the opposite side of *The Debt Checker* is *Working for Debt Calculator,* which determines the total number of hours that must be worked just to pay the interest on all nonmortgage debts without reducing the amount of debt owed. ($3\frac{1}{4}'' \times 8\frac{1}{4}''$).

The Debt Signals Ruler is a quick-and-easy debt reference scale, ruler and bookmark. Use this to do a quick check of the severity level of debt to net income, either with or without mortgage debt. Serves as a 6″ ruler, too. Genesis–The Financial Services Press, 1031 Sanders St., Auburn, AL 36830-2635, 334-826-3238 (both for $10 + $1 for shipping).

INDEX

ABOUT THE AUTHOR

Fred Waddell, PhD, an associate professor at Auburn University, is the author of seven books and training manuals, including *Solution Focused Financial Counseling* (1994) and 135 other publications in the field of financial counseling and family money management. Often referred to as "The Money Doctor," his interviews on money matters have been featured in nationally syndicated news and on radio and television. He has trained over 4,000 consumer credit counselors, financial counselors in credit unions, in the military, in employee assistance programs and therapists.

Dr. Waddell's Solution Focused Financial Counseling is becoming widely recognized as a major development in the field that enables people to resolve financial problems and gain financial control in only one or two counseling sessions. It is being used effectively in financial counseling by telephone.

A human behavior specialist, Certified Master Practitioner in Neuro-Linguistic Programming™ (NLP) and trained in Solution Focused Brief Therapy, he is a nationally recognized expert in helping people eliminate compulsive spending and other attitudes and habits that result in financial problems.

He is married, has two grown children, enjoys whitewater rafting, cross-country skiing and listening to Celtic music, and resides with his wife and two dogs in Auburn, Alabama.

For further information on financial counselor training and for individual counseling, call 334-826-3238.

New
CD-ROM Money Maker Kits
from Dearborn Multimedia

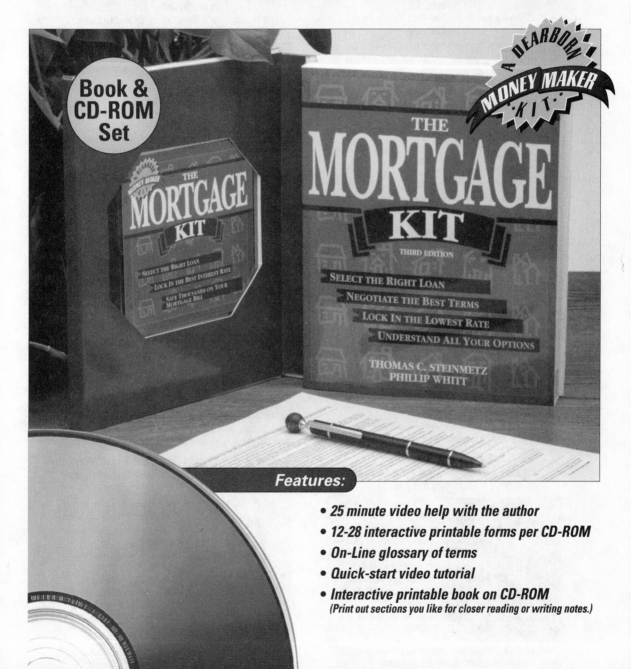

Book & CD-ROM Set

A DEARBORN MONEY MAKER KIT

THE MORTGAGE KIT

SELECT THE RIGHT LOAN
LOCK IN THE BEST INTEREST RATE
SAVE THOUSANDS ON YOUR MORTGAGE BILL

THE MORTGAGE KIT
THIRD EDITION

SELECT THE RIGHT LOAN
NEGOTIATE THE BEST TERMS
LOCK IN THE LOWEST RATE
UNDERSTAND ALL YOUR OPTIONS

THOMAS C. STEINMETZ
PHILLIP WHITT

Features:

- *25 minute video help with the author*
- *12-28 interactive printable forms per CD-ROM*
- *On-Line glossary of terms*
- *Quick-start video tutorial*
- *Interactive printable book on CD-ROM*
  (Print out sections you like for closer reading or writing notes.)

Start Enjoying Greater Financial Freedom
Triple Your Investment Portfolio

SAVE Thousands on Real Estate as a Buyer or Seller

Successfully Start & Manage a **NEW** Business

Small Business

The Business Planning Guide
Plan for Success in Your New Venture

With this multimedia kit:
- Just plug in your financials to plan your dream business
- Point and click to automate planning and financial forecasts
- Start, expand, or buy a business

Over 400,000 Copies Sold!

Order No. 1800-0101
$34.95

David H. Bangs, Jr. is founder of Upstart Publishing Company, Inc.

How To Form Your Own Corporation Without a Lawyer For Under $75

With this multimedia kit:
- Save thousands of dollars in legal fees
- Limit your personal liability and protect your assets
- Access the complete set of forms, certificate of incorporation, minutes, and more

Over 1,000,000 Copies Sold!

Order No. 1800-1601
$34.95

Ted Nicholas owns and operates four corporations of his own and acts as a consultant to small businesses.

Starting Your Home-Based Business
39 Million People Can't Be Wrong

With this multimedia kit:
- Position your home-based business for long-term success
- Deal effectively with zoning, labor laws, and licenses
- Answers to the 20 most-asked questions

Order No. 1800-2801
$34.95

Linda Pinson and **Jerry Jinnett** are consultants and speakers as well as successful business owners and authors.

The Start-Up Guide
Everything You Need to Create a Smart Start in Your New Business

With this multimedia kit:
- Create your own 12-month interactive start-up plan
- Access interactive management, bookkeeping, and marketing forms
- Learn the best ways to deal with bankers, vendors, and investors
- Get the financing you need

Order No. 1800-1001
$34.95

David H. Bangs, Jr. is a frequent speaker and acknowledged expert on small business management topics.

---

3 Easy Ways to Order

1. By Mail:
Mail to:
Dearborn Multimedia
155 N. Wacker Drive
Chicago, IL 60606

2. By FAX:
FAX your order
(with credit card information)
to: 1-312-836-9958

3. By Phone:
Call Toll-Free
(credit card orders only)
1-800-638-0375
Have your Visa, MasterCard, or American Express handy.

Name_____

Address_____ City_____

State_____ Zip_____ Phone (   )_____

❑ Personal Check Enclosed (checks payable to: Dearborn Financial Publishing)
Credit Card Information   ❑ Visa   ❑ MasterCard   ❑ AMEX

Account #_____ Exp. Date_____

Signature_____

Order No.	Title	Price	Qty.	Total

Subtotal	
Sales Tax (CA, FL, IL and NY only)	
Shipping & Handling $5.00	
Total	

Dearborn Multimedia
155 North Wacker Drive
Chicago, IL 60606
1-800-638-0375

Source Code 605118